SPACE ON EARTH

HOW THINKING LIKE AN ASTRONAUT
CAN HELP SAVE THE PLANET

SPACE ON EARTH

HOW THINKING LIKE AN ASTRONAUT CAN HELP SAVE THE PLANET

DR. DAVE WILLIAMS and **LINDA PRUESSEN**

Illustrations by **SHO UEHARA**

annick press
toronto • berkeley

To Bug and Bean, with love to infinity and beyond — LP
To those committed to preserving our planet for future generations — DW

The authors would like to thank Ms. Joanne Arcand, science teacher at the Dr. David R. Williams Public School, for her helpful feedback on the experiments included in this book.

We acknowledge the support of the Canada Council for the Arts and the Ontario Arts Council, and the participation of the Government of Canada/la participation du gouvernement du Canada for our publishing activities.

We would like to acknowledge funding support from the Ontario Arts Council, an agency of the Government of Ontario.

Library and Archives Canada Cataloguing in Publication

Title: Space on Earth : how thinking like an astronaut can help save the planet / Dr. Dave Williams and Linda Pruessen ; illustrated by Sho Uehara.

Names: Williams, Dave (Dafydd Rhys), 1954- author. | Pruessen, Linda, author. | Uehara, Sho, illustrator.

Description: Includes bibliographical references and index.

Identifiers: Canadiana (print) 20220420009 | Canadiana (ebook) 20220420130 | ISBN 9781773217673 (softcover) | ISBN 9781773217666 (hardcover) | ISBN 9781773217680 (HTML) | ISBN 9781773217697 (PDF)

Subjects: LCSH: Environmental protection—Technological innovations—Juvenile literature. | LCSH: Astronautics—Technology transfer—Juvenile literature. | LCSH: Green technology—Juvenile literature. | LCSH: Green technology—Technological innovations—Juvenile literature.

Classification: LCC TD170.15 .W55 2023 | DDC j628.028/4—dc23

Published in the U.S.A. by Annick Press (U.S.) Ltd.
Distributed in Canada by University of Toronto Press.
Distributed in the U.S.A. by Publishers Group West.

Printed in China

annickpress.com • astrodavemd.ca • shouehara.com

Also available as an e-book. Please visit **annickpress.com/ebooks** for more details.

TABLE OF CONTENTS

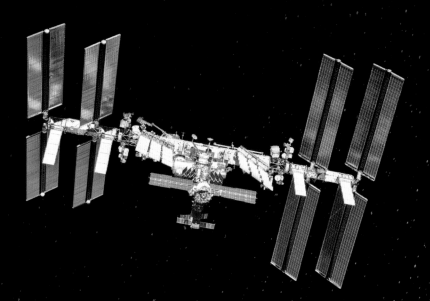

INTRODUCTION

SPACESHIP EARTH

Have you ever seen a photo of the International Space Station (ISS)? It's kind of an odd-looking thing. Picture an insect with really big wings that stick out from a tiny body. Those wings are solar panels that collect energy from the sun, and they make the ISS look pretty big. But actually, the area where the astronauts live and work is small—not even the size of an American football field. That's not a lot of space to house everything astronauts need to live safely and well for months at a time.

No wonder, then, that ever since humans launched themselves into orbit, "sustainability" has been the name of the game for space travel and stays. Astronauts have to protect their resources and their environment because their lives depend on it. They can't open a window to get fresh air because there is no air. They can't pop out to the store to pick up new supplies of water or food. They can't take out the trash. And they can't buy new parts if an important piece of equipment breaks down. They have to take very good care of their home because that space station is their whole world. Pollute the air or water, for example, and someone might get sick (or worse). Run out of power, and the systems that make it possible to live in space will fail.

Planting trees helps keep the air we breathe clean.

Down here on Earth, we think a lot about sustainability, too. Taking care of our environment is a top priority. We know that living unsustainably—using too many fossil fuels, for example, or creating too much garbage—has contributed to climate change. And so, we work hard every day to protect the planet for future generations. We recycle, we turn off the tap when we're brushing our teeth, and we walk to school instead of driving, if we can. We know that the future of the planet depends on actions like these—and that even more needs to be done. Earth's average temperature has risen by about 0.8°C (1.5°F) over the last 100 years. That doesn't sound like a huge change, but it's enough to melt glaciers, cause droughts, and kill off certain species. And the temperature is still rising. Scientists expect it to increase at least another 1.5°C (2.7°F) by 2100.

If that happens, we will find ourselves in trouble that may be too hard to fix. Changing weather patterns will force some people out of their homes due to rising sea levels, forest fires,

Dying coral reefs

or floods. Those same conditions may also make it harder for us to grow the food we need to feed ourselves. And while some species may become extinct (like coral), others may enjoy the warmer temperatures. Mosquitoes, for example, could become a lot more common in many more places—bringing malaria and other diseases with them. It's a pretty scary picture—just as scary, in fact, as what would happen to those astronauts on the ISS if they didn't take care of their environment.

When it comes right down to it, then, our planet isn't so different from the ISS. Think about it as Spaceship Earth. It's bigger than the space station, to be sure, and that size can sometimes make it seem like we have a limitless supply of the resources we need. But the plain truth is that we don't. So maybe it's time to get inspired by the astronauts who live and work in space. How do they keep their air and water clean, and make sure there's enough food to eat? How do they cut down on trash and energy use? Are there ideas being explored in space that could spark innovations in our own backyards? The answer to all of these questions is "Yes!"

Throughout this book, we'll take a closer look at some of the key environmental problems we're facing on Spaceship Earth, and then we'll look up—way up!—for inspiration. By the time you finish reading, one thing will be very clear: there's no shortage of amazing and innovative ideas for protecting this planet we call home.

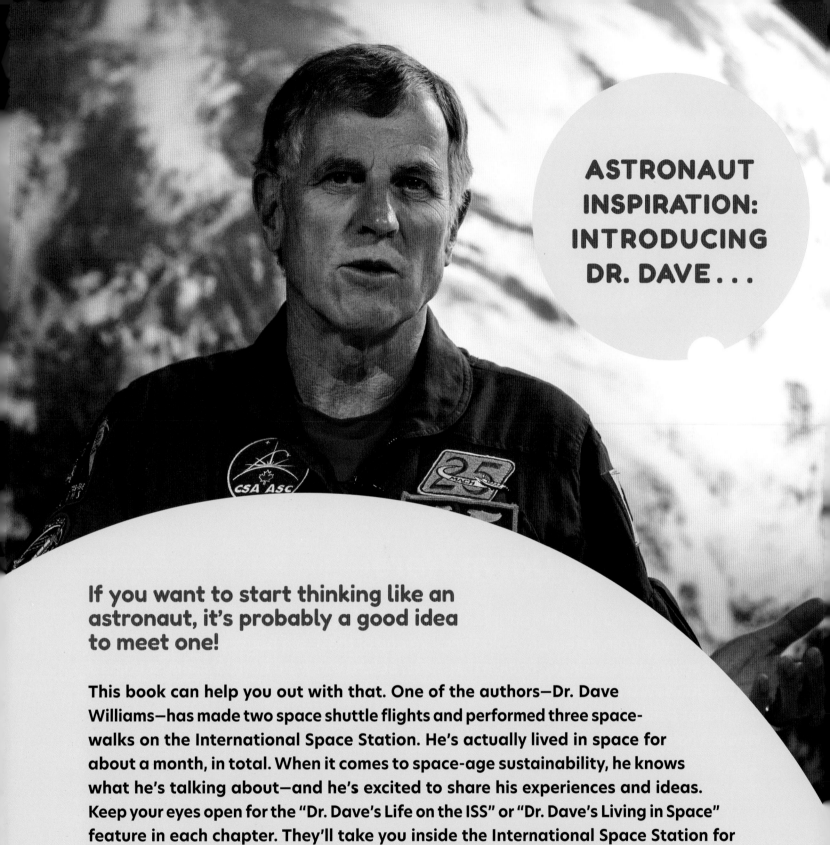

ASTRONAUT INSPIRATION: INTRODUCING DR. DAVE...

If you want to start thinking like an astronaut, it's probably a good idea to meet one!

This book can help you out with that. One of the authors—Dr. Dave Williams—has made two space shuttle flights and performed three space-walks on the International Space Station. He's actually lived in space for about a month, in total. When it comes to space-age sustainability, he knows what he's talking about—and he's excited to share his experiences and ideas. Keep your eyes open for the "Dr. Dave's Life on the ISS" or "Dr. Dave's Living in Space" feature in each chapter. They'll take you inside the International Space Station for an up-close look at how astronauts take care of their environment.

Dr. Dave is also a scientist, so he's included a few experiments that will help bring what you learn to life. Watch for the "Experimenting with Dr. Dave" feature in each chapter.

CHAPTER 1

WATER INSPIRATION
Make Every Drop Count

The Trouble Down Here

Close your eyes and imagine our planet. Got it? Chances are your brain is painting a picture of Earth from outer space—looking like one of those big bouncy balls you played with when you were younger. Back in the 1990s, before you were born, a scientist named Carl Sagan saw a photograph of Earth taken from the space probe *Voyager 1* and gave our planet a nickname: the "pale blue dot." What he saw when he looked at that photo was a whole lot of blue—the blue of our oceans and seas and lakes.

A whopping 71 percent of Earth's surface is covered in water. So there should be plenty to go around, right? Look quickly and it would seem so, but looks can be deceiving. We need to remind ourselves that we don't have a never-ending supply of water, and to start treating it as the precious resource it really is.

The Water Cycle

"Wait a minute," you might be saying. "Something's not adding up. What about the water cycle? Isn't Earth's water constantly recycled?" Okay, you have a point. Water is, in some ways, a pretty renewable resource. That's because the same water evaporates into the sky and falls as rain over and over and over again. So we kind of *do* have a never-ending

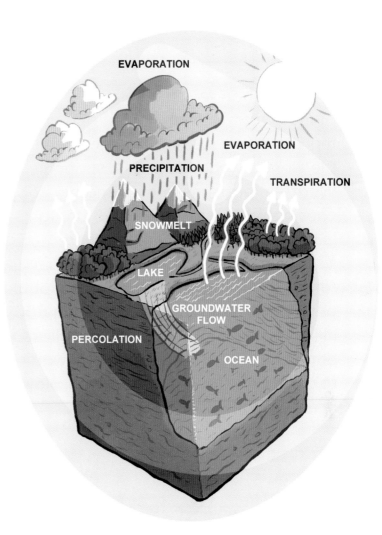

There is the same amount of water on Earth right now as there was when Earth was formed.

If the world's water supply totaled 1 gallon (3.75 liters), the amount of fresh water would be about one third of a cup (80 millimeters). The amount of usable fresh water (the stuff we can access) would be about two to three tablespoons (30-45 milliliters).

supply of water, don't we? Well, yes and no. While we're not likely to run out in the near future, we might soon have a harder time finding water we can actually use.

Supply and Demand

Only 3 percent of all that ancient Earth water is fresh water (not saltwater), and 2.5 percent of that is out of our reach. Some of it is trapped in polar ice caps, glaciers, or soil. And thanks to our growing impact on the planet, a bunch of the water we can access is polluted, making it unsafe to use.

Climate change isn't helping. As the planet warms, rivers, lakes, and aquifers are drying up, and more than half of the world's wetlands have disappeared. Weather patterns are changing, too, causing water shortages and droughts in some areas and floods in others.

And then, of course, there's us—a global population that grew by more than 800 million between 2010 and 2020—all creating an ever-greater demand for water to drink, grow food and cook with, play in and on, and power our industries.

It's a Girl Thing

Women and girls can be especially hard-hit by water scarcity and sanitation issues. In many parts of the world, women are responsible for getting water to the home. In sub-Saharan Africa, for example, women and girls walk an average of 6 kilometers (3.7 miles) hauling 20 kilograms (44 pounds) of water each day. This doesn't leave much energy for other activities, like attending school or working a paid job.

As well, girls who have started menstruating may drop out of school if there is no access to clean water or washrooms. A lack of clean water during childbirth also contributes to high rates of disease.

Down the Drain

A high demand for water coupled with a limited and shrinking supply might be manageable if we were using the water we do have wisely. But many of us are not. The not-so-water-wise leave taps running while they brush their teeth or run the water in the shower for ages before they get in, and they can take their time when it comes to fixing leaky faucets or toilets. And then, there's the water it takes to make all the stuff we use and own. Creating a single pair of jeans, for example, uses about 10,932 liters (2,888 gallons) of water, while producing a 2 liter (0.5 gallon) bottle of soda takes between 680 and 1,242 liters (180 and 328 gallons). That's a whole lot of water going, going, gone.

Add it all up and you've got a global water crisis—what many experts consider to be one of the top 10 threats to our civilization. Some countries don't have enough water to grow the food needed to feed their population. Others struggle to control diseases that show up when unclean water is used for drinking, cooking, and bathing.

And this isn't just a problem in low-income nations. Several U.S. states are facing water shortages, and lack of access to clean drinking water is a big problem in many First Nations communities in Canada. No wonder one of the United Nations' Sustainable Development Goals is to provide universal access to clean water and sanitation by 2030. To make that happen, we need to be much more careful about how we manage our water resources.

BREAKING IT DOWN

1 BILLION people don't have access to clean drinking water

2.7 BILLION find water scarce for at least one month a year

2.4 BILLION people deal with inadequate sanitation

1 MILLION people, mostly children, die each year from illnesses associated with poor water quality and sanitation

BY 2025, two-thirds of the world's population will live in a water-stressed country

Look Up for Inspiration

Up on the International Space Station, 400 kilometers (250 miles) above the planet's surface, astronauts don't worry about giant manufacturing plants polluting their drinking water, or whether climate change is mucking up the world's water supply. But that doesn't mean they don't have to worry about water. In fact, ever since astronauts began living on the ISS, making every drop of water count has been a big concern.

A Precious Resource

In space, astronauts are always aware of just how precious a resource water is. Because there's such a limited supply on board, they tend to use a lot less of it than we do on Earth. But astronauts and Earthlings all need to drink 10 to 14 cups (3 to 4 liters or quarts) of fluids a day to survive. So it's all of the other things we use water for that make a difference.

At home, there are sinks, showers, laundry machines, and maybe hoses to water a garden or wash a car. All of those things work because many of us have "running water," supplied to our homes by the city or town we live in. We turn on a tap or press a button and—presto!—water comes flowing out. In space, there is no running water. Almost all of the water that's on the ISS has to come from home (more on that "almost all" below!), and space up there is limited. Does a rocket have room to shuttle thousands of liters of water to the ISS for a six-month mission? Nope! Does the ISS have room to store it? Also nope! Instead, enough water to last the crew for a few months is brought by cargo vehicle to the ISS in soft-sided waterproof bags. With such a limited water supply on board, astronauts have to make every drop count by remembering the three Rs—reduce, reuse, and recycle.

Reducing: No Showers, No Flushing, No Laundry

Since astronauts can't reduce the amount of water they drink, they have to cut back in other ways. And they've gotten really good at it! The average astronaut is pretty water wise—because they have to be.

There are no sinks or showers and no drains or taps in space. Instead, small water-filled bags are used for brushing teeth, washing, or showering. Without gravity, water sticks to the skin, like a water droplet on a leaf. Some astronauts spread that water around on their skin to wash and then let it evaporate; others use a wet washcloth to clean their body. Rinse-less shampoo keeps astronaut hair clean, and edible toothpaste takes care of teeth in space. And there's no worry about using water for laundry in space because there's no laundry machine. Astronauts wear cotton clothes that are thrown away when dirty.

At the end of each day, an astronaut will have used a little more than 4 liters (1 gallon) of water—and about 90 percent of that is for drinking. Astronauts use every drop of the water they get in order to be efficient, but also because there's no drain like the ones we have at home in sinks and showers, and there's no place to store dirty water!

Now, compare that to what goes on down here. In places where water is easy to access, an average person might use between 302 and 378 liters (80 and 100 gallons) per day! That's *a lot* of water! They aren't drinking more. They're just taking longer showers, using water with every flush of the toilet, washing dishes and clothes when the load isn't full, and watering lawns—all without thinking twice about the resource they are using, and wasting, in the process. Unlike astronauts, most people on Earth drink just 1 percent of the water they use every day.

Reuse and Recycle: The Environmental Control and Life Support System

If you can't bring a bunch of clean water to space from home, and you can't store the dirty water that's created after you use what little you have, what's the solution? Space agencies have gotten creative when it comes to finding every drop of water available on the ISS and turning it into drinking water. And it works!

The ISS recycles about 90 percent of its water, more than 3,785 liters (1,000 gallons) a year. The amazing piece of space technology that gets the job done is the Environmental Control and Life Support System—or ECLSS—which recovers water, revitalizes air, and generates oxygen. For now, let's look at how ECLSS recovers water.

The biggest water hog on Earth is agriculture, which accounts for about 70 percent of our freshwater use.

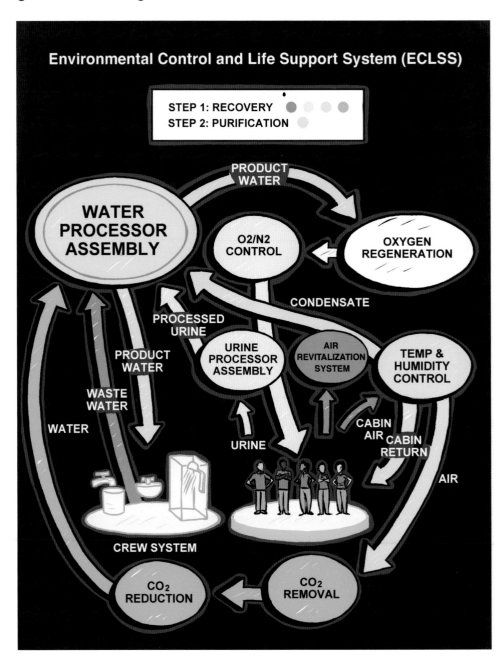

Environmental Control and Life Support System (ECLSS)

STEP 1: RECOVERY
STEP 2: PURIFICATION

PRODUCT WATER

WATER PROCESSOR ASSEMBLY

O2/N2 CONTROL

OXYGEN REGENERATION

CONDENSATE

PROCESSED URINE

PRODUCT WATER

URINE PROCESSOR ASSEMBLY

AIR REVITALIZATION SYSTEM

TEMP & HUMIDITY CONTROL

WASTE WATER

WATER

URINE

CABIN AIR CABIN RETURN

AIR

CREW SYSTEM

CO2 REDUCTION

CO2 REMOVAL

Recovery

STEP 1

The first step in recovering water is collecting it. Inside the ISS, water can be found in many places, if you know where to look. It is in an astronaut's breath when they exhale and in their sweat when they exercise. ECLSS collects those sources of water by working kind of like how a dehumidifier works in your home: water condenses on cool surfaces and is then collected. It can also be found in the hydration systems of the space suits astronauts wear—and, of course, in their pee.

On the ISS, the Universal Waste Management System, or UWMS—a fancy name for a toilet—uses a funnel connected to a suction hose to direct urine to a Urine Processor Assembly (UPA).

Purification

STEP 2

Once the urine is in the UPA, it is pre-treated with powerful acids to reduce the buildup of chemical contaminants and control the growth of microorganisms and fungi. The water from the UPA is then combined with the other wastewater that's been recovered and is delivered to the Water Processor Assembly (WPA), which removes gas, hair, and lint before sending the water along to filtration beds for further purification. The final step is a reactor assembly that uses a high temperature and chemicals to remove any remaining contaminants and microorganisms. The mixture of calcium, salt, and other compounds removed from the water during purification is gathered into a bladder and stored, and then either discarded or returned to Earth to be studied. Just to be sure the water is pure, it is checked with special sensors, and any unacceptable water is sent back to be reprocessed.

Is 100 Percent Possible?

It's pretty amazing that 90 percent of the water on the ISS is recycled, but can that figure go higher? Is 100 percent possible? It's hard to imagine. Currently, black water (contaminated with human waste) and gray water (contaminated with bacteria) are discarded. But NASA and other space agencies around the world are working on finding solutions. Perhaps one day a truly "closed system" for water recycling—a system where absolutely nothing is wasted—will be available for use in space and on Earth.

Storage and Reuse

STEP 3

After a quick final check, the clean water is sent to a storage tank for the crew to use. Yesterday's wastewater—and pee—is now totally safe to use for bathing, brushing teeth, rehydrating food, or even drinking. No wonder astronauts sometimes joke that today's coffee will become tomorrow's coffee!

DR. DAVE'S LIVING IN SPACE

Soap, Shampoo, and a Vacuum?

Ask astronauts what they miss most about Earth when they are in space, and you might hear "a long, hot shower!"

About 50 years ago, the first NASA space station, called Skylab, had a shower—a long cylinder of water-resistant material that sealed at both ends when someone was inside. Astronauts could squirt several cups of water over their body using a handheld water dispenser and then lather up with soap. That's when things got complicated. Since there was no gravity to help direct the soapy water down a drain, a handheld vacuum was used to suck up that lather before toweling dry!

Skylab was the last space station to have a shower. My astronaut training included "toilet training" (yes, that's what they actually call it on the schedule!) and briefings on how to bathe with a wet towel and rinse-less shampoo. By the time I arrived in space, I knew how to stay clean without using much water. But after a few weeks, I was definitely dreaming about a real shower.

Space on Earth

Using as little water as possible. Recycling what is used. Being creative when it comes to finding sources. That's what happens on the ISS because astronauts know their water supply isn't limitless. Down here on Earth, we're also treating our water with care—and we're looking to space for new ideas.

Cleaning Up the Mess

In regions of the world where water is scarce, clean drinking water can be hard to find—and as we saw on page 13, drinking water that isn't clean can cause illness and death. In some places, the same type of purification technology used on the ISS is being used to help make sure everyone has access to clean water.

- In 2006, the nonprofit organization Concern for Kids learned about a well failure in northern Iraq. The village of Kendala had once been home to about 1,000 people, but with no access to drinking water, many moved away. The 150 or so who stayed were using contaminated water from a nearby creek. Working with the Water Security Corporation, Concern for Kids helped to install a water-filtration system based on NASA technology—and for the first time in two years, Kendala had clean, safe drinking water.

- In the rural community of Chiapas, Mexico, clean drinking water is hard to come by—and waterborne illnesses are common. In 2013, an ECLSS-style water-purification plant—powered by renewable solar energy—was installed. With clean water now available at the local school, fewer children are suffering from parasites and stomach bugs, and the whole community is healthier. There are economic advantages, too, as families don't need to buy as much purified water or medication to treat illnesses.

In Canada's Far North, one bed-and-breakfast owner in Iqaluit, Nunavut, took water recycling and purification to the next level. In 1999, Jens Steenberg installed a biofilter in his sewage tank. Like the system on the ISS, Steenberg's system was all about recycling and reusing, but his system put naturally occurring bacteria to work to get rid of solid waste. Once the solid waste was gone, the system filtered what was left, disinfected it with ozone, and sent the treated gray water back into the B&B's plumbing system, where Steenberg used it to wash clothes and flush toilets. In the Arctic, where both water and sewage treatment are expensive, a system like this could be a game changer; it cut Steenberg's water usage by 60 percent and drastically reduced the need for sewage pickup.

No Water Required

On the ISS, astronauts try to use as little water as possible. Even their toilets get the job done without a tank—which is a pretty big deal considering that the average toilet flushes about 30 percent of our at-home water use straight down the drain. Entrepreneurs are hard at work on developing a waterless toilet for the rest of us, too. Not only will the technology save water, but it may keep us from getting sick.

Microsoft founder Bill Gates is all-in on this idea. In 2018, he even hosted a "Reinvented Toilet Expo" to bring together people interested in creating toilets that don't rely on water and do remove the harmful parts of human waste—the bacteria and parasites that can make us so sick if they get into our water supply. There are lots of designs out there, but most involve a system that separates waste, cleans it, and stores it for disposal. That isn't ideal on the ISS, and it creates extra steps and energy use here on Earth, too. Luckily, more ideas are being developed every day.

In water-stressed Madagascar, for example, a very water-friendly toilet is already in use. Developed in England, the Loowatt toilet doesn't need water or a sewer system to work. A biodegradable bag simply stores waste under the toilet until it can be picked up and sent to a "biodigester," which turns it into liquid fertilizer, compost, or even electricity. Virginia Gardiner, whose company developed the Loowatt, believes the toilet can help other places like Madagascar where water and sanitation issues are common. But there's an opportunity for change else-where, too. In the United Kingdom, the Loowatt is available for rent to use during public events. Given how much water each flush takes, just imagine how much can be saved by not flushing at all.

Eyes in the Sky

So far, we've learned a lot about how water conservation efforts on the ISS can inspire us to be even more water wise on Earth. But when it comes to taking care of this precious resource, Earth is getting a bit of extra help from space, too. Since 1957, when the Soviet Union launched Sputnik 1, thousands of satellites have been sent into space to gather information about Earth, its atmosphere, and outer space. In 2020, thousands of satellites were in orbit, helping us make phone calls, tune in to our favorite television shows, gather information about clouds or oceans or the polar ice caps, or measure gases in the atmosphere. Some are also helping with our water woes.

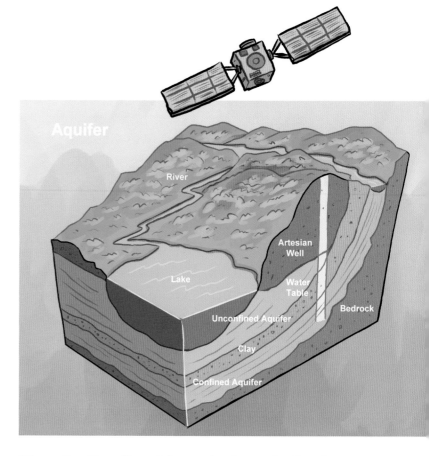

"Unconfined" aquifers sit beneath a layer of soil and can be reached by wells and pumps. "Confined" aquifers are trapped between solid layers of rock.

Scientists believe that aquifers—layers of rock or sediment that hold groundwater beneath Earth's surface—contain between 30 and 40 percent of all the liquid fresh water on Earth. And we don't hesitate to help ourselves to that hidden supply. Groundwater is often used to help water crops and supply nearby cities, especially in places that don't get enough rain. In California, for example, 38 percent of the state's water supply comes from aquifers. And in India, about 80 percent of the country's 1.35 billion people rely on groundwater for drinking and farming.

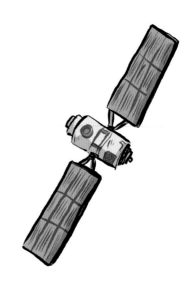

In 2002, NASA and the German Aerospace Center launched two satellites as part of the Gravity Recovery and Climate Experiment—or GRACE. Every 30 days, the satellites mapped Earth's gravity field, looking for changes that could provide information about polar ice sheets, ocean currents, Earth's interior, and the water cycle. As well as measuring changes in the water supply aboveground, GRACE sensed the levels of the water stored in aquifers. In 2015, a study at the University of California, Irvine, used GRACE data to warn that 21 of the world's 37 largest aquifers were being depleted or were in distress. That information can help governments make better decisions when it comes to managing water supply.

Satellites have been keeping their eyes on our water in other ways, too.

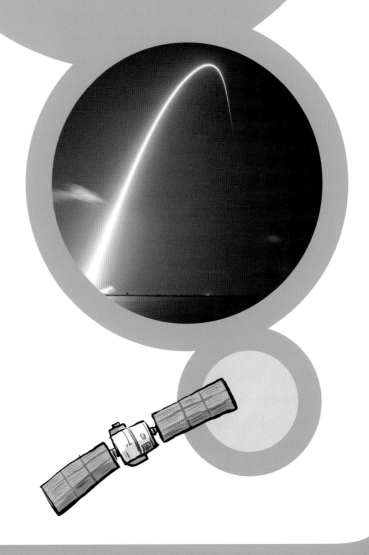

- Satellite data has been used to help find places where groundwater is close to the surface. Being able to dig a well with hand tools instead of a high-tech mechanical drill can make a huge difference in some places.

- Satellite data can help determine water quality by measuring the amount of algae present (algae feeds on sewage).

- Satellite data can be used to identify leaks in water supply systems, helping to make sure that not a drop is wasted.

With all those satellites orbiting Earth, who knows what else they'll be able to help us with in the future?

Spot the Satellite

While some satellites are too far above Earth's surface to be seen, others can be spotted in the night sky. On a clear night, find a place away from very bright lights—a backyard or a nearby park will do. Then, look up. The first thing you'll notice are the stars and then maybe an airplane or two. Planes have flashing or blinking lights and move along pretty quickly. Keep your eyes open for a small, steady light traveling slowly and steadily across the sky. Sometimes, they even travel in "trains," like the Starlink satellite network pictured below. It was launched by SpaceX in 2019 as part of a plan to beam the Internet to Earth from space.

Think Like an Astronaut

It could be a while before a waterless toilet makes its way to your house, but don't let that stop you: there are lots of ways you can "think like an astronaut" and make every drop count.

Turn Off the Tap

Do you leave the tap running when you brush your teeth? Turn it off instead. Letting the water run while you brush and rinse can waste 15 liters (4 gallons) of water. Multiply that by two (the average number of times a person brushes each day) and then by four (for an average-sized family), and you've got 120 liters (32 gallons) of water wasted in one house every single day. Keep an eye open for a leaky faucet, too: a faucet that drips just three times a minute wastes 1.6 liters (0.4 gallons) of water a day, or around 600 liters (160 gallons) a year. That's about three full rain barrels, just from one house!

Jump in the Shower

If you're a fan of long, hot baths, consider giving showers a chance. An efficient showerhead uses about 7.5 liters (2 gallons) of water each minute. This means that a 10-minute shower uses 75 liters (20 gallons) of water. By comparison, filling a bathtub uses about 185 liters (50 gallons). As long as you're not taking 25-minute showers, you'll be saving some water. You can also challenge yourself to shower like a sailor—on a sailboat, usable water is about as limited as it is in space. Use only enough water to wet yourself, turn off the water, soap up, and then turn the water back on to rinse off. Then feel good about caring for yourself and the planet.

Wait for a Full Load

If laundry is one of your household chores, here's a useful tip (and if it isn't, why not volunteer to help?): don't run the machine until you have a full load. Some washing machines use up to 70 liters (18.5 gallons) of water for each load of laundry. An average of five loads a week for a full year means 18,200 liters (4,800 gallons) of water, just to clean your clothes. Waiting until there are enough clothes to fill the machine can cut down on the number of loads—and the amount of water used.

Energy-efficient washing machines can reduce that by 33 percent, saving about 6,000 liters (1,585 gallons) of water a year.

Drink Water Instead of Juice

This might seem like a strange tip for saving water, but check this out: it takes about 1,000 liters (265 gallons) of water to grow and produce 1 liter (1 quart) of orange juice, while it takes about 1,140 liters (250 gallons) to produce the same amount of apple juice. So, next time you're thirsty, why not reach for a tall, cool glass of plain water. It's good for you and good for the environment.

Put Rain to Good Use

Instead of using tap water for the lawn and garden, go with nature's choice—rainwater. A rain barrel, or even an old bucket or two, in your yard or on your balcony will catch water when it rains. Then, when the weather is dry, you can use that water to keep plants healthy. Depending on where you live, you could save about 5,000 liters (1,100 gallons) of tap water.

EXPERIMENTING WITH DR. DAVE

Build Your Own Water Purifier

You've learned about water purification on the ISS and seen how the technology is making a difference in water-stressed areas around the world. Building a simple solar distiller can show you one type of water purification in action.

You'll need:

- two identical plastic bottles with plastic caps (500 mL/16 oz. or 1 L/1 qt. work best)
- a hand drill with a 1/4" (about 5 mm) or similar-size drill bit, and an adult who can operate it
- hot glue or duct tape
- salt
- food coloring (or if you have some used-up markers, use the felt inside the markers to color the water)
- a brick, piece of wood, or emply box
- a black garbage bag (optional)

1 Stand the two bottles upright and make sure the caps are screwed on tight.

2 Poke a hole through each cap (ask an adult for help with the drill) so there will be an opening between the two bottles when they are connected.

3 Glue or tape the tops of the caps together so the two bottles can be attached end to end.

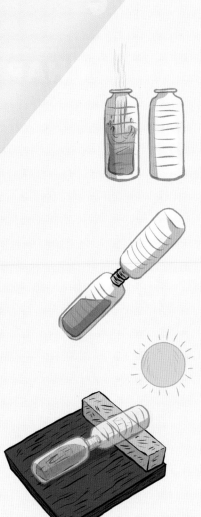

4   Remove the caps from the bottles. Fill one bottle about half full with water. Add 4 drops of foodcoloring and a tablespoon of salt to represent contaminants in the water.

5   Attach the caps to that bottle, and then screw the empty bottle on top of the other cap.

6   Go outside on a sunny day. Place a brick, a piece of wood, or an empty box on a table or the ground and use it to raise the empty end of the bottles at an angle with the partially full bottle resting on the ground.

7   Over time*, the water in the lower bottle will evaporate and condense in the upper bottle as clear, fresh water. If you were to have this water tested, chances are it would be clean enough to drink.

* It may take a while to collect the water. Try covering the bottle with the colored water with a black garbage bag to see if it speeds up the process.

CHAPTER 2

AIR INSPIRATION

Keep It Clean

The Trouble Down Here

Air is a funny thing. We can't see it, but it's all around us—whether we're standing on a city street, out in a wide green field, on the top of a mountain, or even inside the International Space Station. And that's a good thing, because we (and every other living thing on the planet) need it to survive.

We also need for it to be clean—for our own health and for the health of the planet. Right now, though, the air we're breathing every day on Earth isn't so clean. Air pollution is a big problem, and we need to work harder to clean up our act.

What the Heck *Is* Air, Anyway?

To understand how harmful pollution can be, we need to understand air—specifically, what should and shouldn't be in it. So let's break that down. Air is mostly made up of gases: about 78 percent nitrogen, 21 percent oxygen, and 1 percent of a bunch of other things (like carbon dioxide, neon, and hydrogen). Hanging around with those gases are tiny particles of stuff. Many of these particles—called aerosols—are natural and pretty harmless: think dust and pollen, for example. They might make your nose run if you have allergies, but for most people, they aren't a big problem.

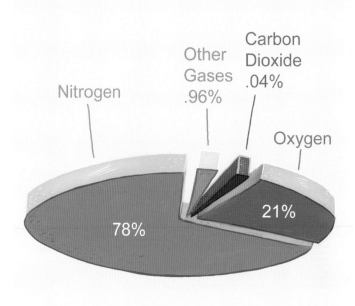

Unfortunately, not all aerosols are created equal. Some are formed when fossil fuels are burned, when cars, trucks, and factories spew exhaust, and when wildfires rage. Those aerosols muck up our air with soot and smoke.

The worst levels of air pollution in southern California were recorded during a devastating wildfire in September 2020.

Take carbon dioxide, a.k.a. CO_2. Humans and animals breathe in oxygen and give off CO_2. It's a necessary gas and a normal part of our air—plants use it to feed themselves (through photosynthesis) and to produce oxygen that humans and plants need. But the large amount of CO_2 that is currently in the air because of pollution from cars and power plants is *not* necessary,

The Air Quality Index

The idea that poor air quality can make us sick isn't a big secret. All over the world, environmental agencies measure air quality so they can warn us when pollution is reaching dangerous levels. To do this, they use an air quality index (AQI) that features numbers and colors. The air quality is measured on a scale, that varies depending on where you live. In the United States, for example, it goes from 0 (green) to 500 (maroon); in Canada, it starts at 1 (blue) and goes to 10+ (maroon). What doesn't change, though, is that the lower the number, the better. In the United States, if the AQI is higher than 100, you should probably stay inside. Breathing the air outdoors would be like breathing in the exhaust from a car all day long.

You can find the air quality index for your area on a weather channel, an environmental agency website, or by typing "AQI" plus the name of your city or town into a search engine.

(0-50)	(51-100)	(101-150)	(151-200)	(201-300)
GOOD	MODERATE	UNHEALTHY FOR SENSITIVE GROUPS	UNHEALTHY	VERY UNHEALTHY

and definitely not good. In fact, this greenhouse gas is the most important contributor to human-caused global warming.

And then there's ozone. Up high in the atmosphere, ozone is a good thing—it forms a protective layer that shields Earth from the full strength of the sun's rays. Closer to the ground, though, it's bad news. When particles in the air combine with ozone, they create smog.

Whether from aerosols or another source, pollution affects the quality of the air we breathe, and it can make us sick. That's bad enough, but all of that yuck also makes its way back down to Earth—and into our water and soil—when small amounts of water in the air build up and are released in the form of raindrops. There's no doubt about it: pollution is a problem.

The Problem with Pollution

There are *a lot* of problems with air pollution, but we're going to focus on two:

AIR POLLUTION MAKES US SICK

All that stuff that's floating around in the air and shouldn't be is a major cause of death and disease. Lung cancer, heart disease, stroke, and respiratory infections like pneumonia can all be caused or worsened by poor air quality. When pregnant women are exposed to pollution, their babies can be born too early or with low birth weights. And in children under the age of five, almost half of deaths due to pneumonia are caused by soot breathed in from household air pollution. This is a big concern in parts of the world where families often cook over open stoves.

AIR POLLUTION MAKES THE PLANET SICK

You probably know a thing or two about greenhouse gases (GHGs) like carbon dioxide, ozone, and methane. They get a lot of bad press these days, but GHGs are actually a good news/bad news kind of story. Most of them occur naturally and can have a beneficial effect in the right doses (think about how ozone protects us from the sun's radiation, for example). But too much of a good thing can be . . . well . . . bad. For the past 200 years or so, ever since we began relying on fossil fuels to power our industries and our lives, human-generated GHGs have been

building up in Earth's atmosphere—and getting up to no good. By trapping heat relatively close to Earth's surface, they act as the main contributors to climate change. Think extreme temperatures, rising sea levels or drought, damage to ecosystems and food supplies, and a whole bunch of other problems that have dire consequences for the well-being of the planet and all that call it home.

It can be hard to think about air as something we need to protect. Like with the water we talked about in chapter 1, it can sometimes seem as if we have an endless supply. But there's no doubt that Earth's air pollution problem is real—and really dangerous. Air may be all around us, but we have to do our part to keep it clean. Miles above Earth, astronauts on the ISS have been coming up with inspiring ways to do that for decades.

BREAKING IT DOWN

91 PERCENT of the world's population live in places where air quality guidelines are not met.

93 PERCENT of the world's children under the age of 15—about 1.8 billion kids—are at risk for poor health and development because of poor air quality.

INDOOR AIR POLLUTION—from cooking fires, for example—can be more harmful than pollution outside.

THE CITY WITH THE WORST AIR POLLUTION in the United States is Los Angeles, California; in Canada, it's Windsor, Ontario.

AS OF JULY 2021, the amount of CO_2 in the air was the highest it's ever been, and the seven warmest years on record since 1880 have all occurred since 2014.

Look Up for Inspiration

For astronauts living or traveling in space, a constant supply of air is just as important as it is to us on Earth. And while making sure the air is fresh and clean is a big challenge, an even bigger one is making sure there's air at all.

No Air Up There

Earth has air because it has an atmosphere—a layer of gases that protects life and helps it to survive. But the farther you get from the planet, the thinner that atmosphere gets. That's because the gravity that keeps us all from floating off into space loses its power to hold together the gas molecules that make up our air. Travel 10,000 kilometers (6,214 miles) away from Earth's surface, and those molecules are so far apart that "air" as we know it no longer exists. You're officially in the "exosphere," or what's often called the "vacuum" of space. For humans to live inside a spacecraft or the space station, the air inside must be created, monitored, and replenished. Any glitch in the system and lives are at risk.

How to Breath with No Air: Air Supply on the ISS

The International Space Station gets some of the oxygen on board from Earth. Astronauts bring it with them when they travel to the ISS for a mission, and it also arrives on cargo ships. But it's not enough. If the crews aboard the ISS relied only on oxygen sent from Earth, they'd run out—and that would be bad news. To prevent a shortage of safe, breathable air, the ISS needs to recycle.

Back in chapter 1, we saw how the Environmental Control and Life Support System (ECLSS) helped to supply clean drinking water on the ISS by recycling water from other sources. Another big part of the system's job is to recycle and supply air. An important part of ECLSS is the Oxygen Generation System, which produces oxygen for the crew to breathe by using a process called electrolysis. It works like this:

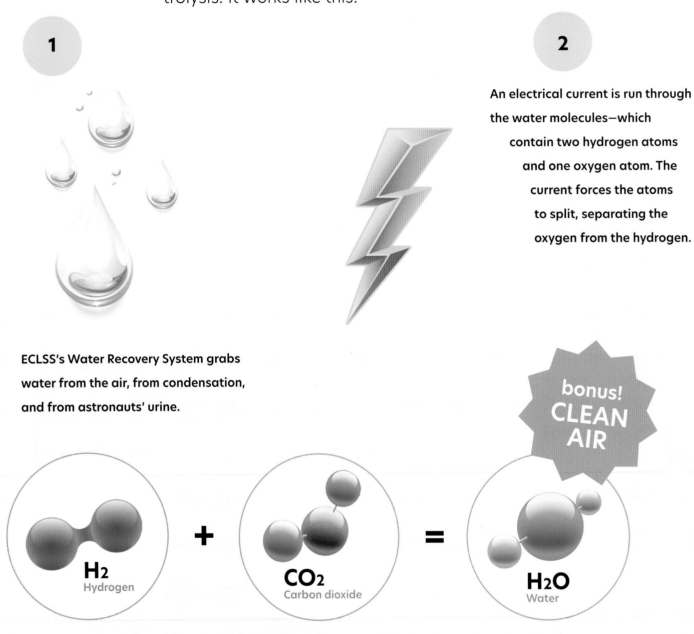

1

ECLSS's Water Recovery System grabs water from the air, from condensation, and from astronauts' urine.

2

An electrical current is run through the water molecules—which contain two hydrogen atoms and one oxygen atom. The current forces the atoms to split, separating the oxygen from the hydrogen.

bonus!
CLEAN
AIR

H_2
Hydrogen

+

CO_2
Carbon dioxide

=

H_2O
Water

H_2 [molecular structure of hydrogen] + CO_2 [molecular structure of carbon dioxide] = H_2O [molecular structure of water]

3 The leftover hydrogen is combined with the CO_2 that the astronauts produce when they breathe. The process creates much-needed water and removes excess CO_2 from the air (too much can make us sick). However, it also produces methane, which is not needed on the ISS and can also make us sick. The methane is sent out into space through vents.

Clean Sweep

In 1970, the Apollo 13 crew found themselves in a life-threatening situation. An oxygen tank exploded in the spacecraft's command module, forcing the three astronauts to move into the much smaller lunar module for the trip home. Once there, a new problem quickly popped up: dangerous levels of CO_2 in the air. Relying on their training and the materials at hand, the astronauts created a filtration system using duct tape, plastic bags, and a tube sock. The Apollo 13 story has a happy ending—everyone made it home safe and sound—but it shows just how important clean air is to life.

In addition to creating some of the air that astronauts aboard the ISS breathe, the Environmental Control and Life Support System also contains the filtration and treatment technology needed to keep that air clean and safe. It includes a system that filters excess carbon dioxide, another system that removes contaminants, and yet *another* system that monitors the levels of the different gases in the air. That's a lot of technology hard at work!

An International Effort

Creating breathable air in space takes cooperation, just like it does on Earth. In the United States, NASA developed the Oxygen Generation System that's currently at work on the ISS. Meanwhile, the European Space Agency has developed a system that converts carbon dioxide into oxygen and water. It can generate about 50 percent of the water needed for oxygen production on the space station and was sent to space on Japan's HTV-7 spacecraft in 2018. The Russian-built Elektron-VM also uses electrolysis to produce oxygen. These systems, and others that are being developed around the world, will be a huge part of life in space as humans go farther and farther from Earth.

Is it possible that there's a less high-tech solution to the problem? On Earth, nature has created its own ECLSS. Forests and plants remove carbon dioxide from the air, create oxygen, and also help to remove contaminants. NASA has been studying the air-purification benefits of plants for decades now, so it's possible that one day plant power will be used on the ISS to help keep the air clean.

Crew members from the USS Iwo Jima recovery ship hoist aboard the Command Module from Apollo 13.

Look Out for Leaks!

A big part of any recycling or sustainability plan is avoiding waste. The ISS crew tries to make sure that as much carefully created and cleaned air stays on board as possible, but it's not always easy. The stuff keeps escaping! Every time the astronauts perform a spacewalk, 9 cubic meters (300 cubic feet) of air is released into space through the airlock. To picture what that looks like, imagine a cylindrical room that's about 1.5 meters (5 feet) in diameter, with a ceiling that is 3 meters (10 feet) high. It's probably bigger than your closet, but not quite as big as your bedroom. Now, imagine all of the air being sucked out of that room and replaced, every time you come in and out. That's a pretty big "leak," but smaller ones happen, too.

Back in 2019, the crew aboard the ISS realized they had a small leak. At the time, it was responsible for the loss of about 0.27 kilograms (0.6 pounds) of air per day—which didn't have anyone too worried. By mid-2020, though, the leak had gotten bigger. Now, 1.4 kilograms (3.1 pounds) of air were escaping, and it was definitely time to fix the problem. But how do you find a small leak on a big space station? You put microgravity to work! The crew released tea leaves into the module where they suspected the leak to be and waited to see where they went. When the leaves began to cluster around a scratch in the wall near some communications equipment, the mystery was solved!

DR. DAVE'S LIFE ON THE ISS

The Sound of Life

Whether you're out on a space-walk or floating around inside the space station, the sound of fans is the sound of life in space. Circulation is an important part of revitalizing the air on the ISS. Some astronauts experience headaches and nausea when working in poorly ventilated parts of the space station, as they use up oxygen and breathe out carbon dioxide, which builds up around them. To help improve air flow, astronauts use portable fans throughout the space station. During my training, I was taught all about this, so I always made sure to work in well-ventilated areas or to have a small fan nearby. No headaches or stomachaches!

Space on Earth

Whether on the International Space Station, in a space suit on a moonwalk, or in a future habitat on Mars, a constant and clean supply of air is essential. It's no wonder, then, that research into how we can supply air and keep it clean in space is always on the go. New technologies are being developed all the time, especially as space agencies consider longer voyages and longer stays. On Earth, we're also constantly exploring new ways to keep our air clean and safe—some of which are inspired by life in space.

The World's Largest Air Purifier

Keeping the air clean on the ISS is hard enough, so how do you do it for an entire city? That's what researchers in Xi'an, China, were trying to figure out back in 2015 when they built an air purification tower 100 meters (328 feet) tall—thought to be the largest such structure in the world.

The tower works by sucking air into a series of greenhouses at the tower's base, where it is heated using solar energy. The warm air then rises through filters inside the tower before it is released. So far, it's working. Researchers report that the tower is putting 10 million cubic meters (353 million cubic feet) of clean air back into the atmosphere each day. They also report that smog levels have dropped from hazardous to moderate levels in a 10-square-kilometer (3.8-square-mile) section of the city around the tower. Plans for much bigger towers in other cities are now in the works.

Air purification projects are getting the green light in other countries, too. In Delhi, India—a city with dangerously high levels of air pollution—a new "smog tower" has been installed in the Lajpat Nagar market. About 15,000 people visit Lajpat Nagar each day, and the tower is expected to purify the area within 500 to 750 meters (1,640 to 2,460 feet) of the market. Smog towers have also been installed in the Netherlands, Poland, and South Korea.

Plant Power!

Trees and plants have an amazing superpower: by breathing in CO_2 and breathing out oxygen, they act as nature's air purifiers. NASA knows this, which is why the space agency has been studying plant power for decades. But cities are getting in on the act now, too, and are looking to plants to help solve the problem of air pollution.

In Italy, China, the Netherlands, Singapore, and other countries, architects and urban planners are creating "vertical forests" to help clean the air. Picture an apartment or office building covered in shrubs and trees, and you get the idea. In China, the Nanjing Vertical Forests are expected to absorb 23,000 kilograms (25 tons) of CO_2 each day, while also producing 60 kilograms (132 pounds) of oxygen—oxygen that happens to be 3,000 times more pure than the city's typical air. To help you figure out what this

South America's Amazon rainforest is often called the "lungs of the planet," and it's been said that the forest produces 20 percent of the oxygen in Earth's atmosphere. That's not technically true, but the Amazon does suck a whole lot of CO_2 out of the atmosphere—which makes it a key player in battling climate change.

means, it's useful to know that one medium-sized family car produces 22,000 kilograms (24 tons) of CO_2 over the course of its entire life!

Meanwhile, in Germany, CityTree is doing the same thing on a smaller scale. CityTree looks like a billboard—the kind that would advertise gum, shampoo, or the latest blockbuster movie. But instead of a glossy ad trying to sell you something, this billboard is filled with moss and lichen. Each CityTree installation can suck in about 220,000 kilograms (240 tons) of CO_2 a year, which does the work of about 275 trees while taking up much less space. It's a handy solution for busy cities where green space is hard to come by and pollution levels are high.

Personal Air Purifiers to the Rescue

Massive smog towers like the ones in China and India are doing great work in cities around the world, but smaller air purifiers can also be big clean-air heroes—just ask the residents of the Porter Ranch community near Los Angeles, California. In 2015 and 2016, a natural gas leak forced thousands of residents out of their homes and even caused two schools to be relocated. It just so happened that a company in the area was distributing the Aerus Air Scrubber

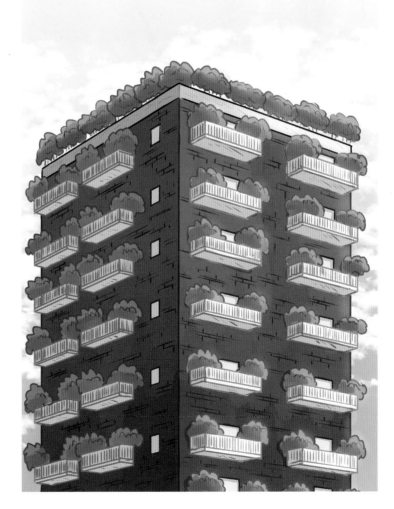

Plus, a device that used NASA-developed technology to purify air and surfaces. The gas company ordered 10,000 of the purifiers and installed them in nearby homes, allowing many residents to stay put.

The purifier uses a process called photocatalytic oxidation—which is a fancy way of saying that it harnesses energy from ultraviolet light to "zap" pollutants and turn them into harmless substances instead. But there's a bonus: photocatalytic oxidation also eliminates bacteria, viruses, and molds. A number of Major League Baseball teams, including the Texas Rangers, are now using the technology in their locker rooms and gyms to prevent outbreaks of contagious infections, and hospitals and hotel rooms are battling bacteria in the same way. Even restaurant kitchens are using the technology to help get rid of exhaust smoke from the stoves.

And to think, it all started because NASA was looking for a way to get rid of ethylene—a gas that builds up on the ISS and makes fruit and veggies ripen too fast.

Keeping an Eye on Pollution

Air purification systems help astronauts stay healthy in space, and they have benefits for human health on Earth, too. But what about the planet? In chapter 1, we saw how satellites are helping us track water levels in Earth's aquifers. Turns out they're also busy monitoring pollution levels.

In 2017, the European Space Agency launched Sentinel-5P, thought to be the world's most advanced pollution-monitoring satellite. It circles the planet 14 times a day, collecting information on gases that affect our air quality.

Space agencies aren't the only ones getting in on the act. Satellites sent into orbit by a Canadian company called GHGSat are on the lookout for emissions from particular buildings, helping us to zoom in on big polluters. And in 2024, the United States plans to launch GeoCarb—the Geostationary Carbon Observatory. From its position 35,800 kilometers (22,236 miles) above Earth, it will keep a close eye on CO_2, methane, and carbon monoxide emissions in the Americas.

The information these satellites send back to Earth is important in helping scientists understand how greenhouse gases affect our atmosphere. That's important all on its own, but there's another benefit to having this many eyes in the sky. Having an accurate picture of where pollution comes from could help make sure that countries and corporations keep their promises to reduce harmful emissions.

Cleaning the Air *under* the Earth

Could small-scale air purifiers be used to clean the air under the earth as well as above it? Mining companies sure think so.

Deep under Earth's surface, miners use heavy equipment and dynamite blasts to extract diamonds, coal, silver, and other valuable natural resources from Earth's crust. But mining is dangerous work. Cave-ins and tunnel collapses are common, and the explosions can cause gas leaks. Even if miners survive a catastrophe, the buildup of carbon dioxide in the air can make it difficult to survive until a rescue team arrives. About 12,000 people a year die in mining accidents.

When the Mine Safety and Health Administration in the United States heard about some of the work NASA was doing to create small air purifiers for future space travel, they thought it might be useful for miners, too. Now, thanks to a Kentucky-based company called Mine Shield, LLC, "refuge chambers" featuring CO_2 "scrubbers" are available to the mining community. Government departments are also considering the technology for use in safe rooms where officials are taken during threats to national security.

Think Like an Astronaut

We're luckier than astronauts: we have air all around us, so we don't need to worry about creating it. But we *absolutely* need to continue paying attention to what we have and keeping it clean. There are lots of ways we can do that.

Plant a Tree

Like the air revitalization system on the ISS, Earth's amazing trees remove CO_2, carbon monoxide, and other gaseous pollutants from the air. In one year, an acre of mature trees can gobble up the amount of carbon monoxide produced by a car trip of 42,000 kilometers (26,000 miles). Why not ask for a tree to be planted for your next birthday or organize a tree planting day in your neighborhood?

Be Energy Efficient

About 60 percent of the electricity produced in the United States comes from fossil fuels, so decreasing the amount of electricity we use is a great way to help keep our air clean. Try turning lights, computers, and gaming systems off when you're not using them; consider drying your clothes on a line instead of in the dryer; and ask your parents about switching to energy-efficient LED light bulbs or appliances.

Take the Bus

One-third of greenhouse gas emissions comes from transportation. If you can't walk or bike to where you're going, consider taking a bus instead—or, if you can, an electric bus. It's estimated that 1,000 electric buses can reduce the use of fossil fuel from 500 barrels a day to just 15. In the United States, communities with good public transportation systems can reduce their carbon emissions by 41 million tons each year. To match that result, every household in New York City, Atlanta, Denver, Los Angeles, and Washington, DC, combined would have to completely stop using electricity.

Be a Fan of the Fan

When it's hot and sticky outside, many of us rely on air conditioners to keep us cool. But maybe we shouldn't. Most air conditioners use gases in cooling loops (like in a refrigerator) that can ruin the ozone layer, and use a bunch of electricity, too. There are better options. Dehumidifiers remove water from the air, which can make it feel cooler. And fans are really good at cooling you off. Wet a washcloth with cool water, wipe your arms and legs, and then stand in front of a fan. Ahh . . . The evaporation of the water from your skin creates a soothing, cooling effect.

Open the Window

One of the best ways to help clean the air in your home might also be the easiest: open a window! Opening windows for just five minutes a day can help you get rid of harmful pollution in your indoor air. Where does that pollution come from? Everywhere! Your shoes track in pesticides, pollen, and even animal poop; some household cleaners contain toxic chemicals; and dark, damp places like bathrooms can be the perfect home for mold. So, crack that window and let the dirty air out.

Peeking at Pollution

Sometimes, it's easy to see air pollution: smoke billows out of stacks at factories, or clouds of exhaust puff out of older cars and trucks. Most of the time, though, the air seems to be clean and fresh. But is it? For this experiment, you'll need a clear plastic container with a wide opening and some petroleum jelly. (You could have your parents help you cut the top off a plastic bottle from the experiment in chapter 1 and use the bottom).

1   Using your fingers, a brush, or a cloth, spread a thin layer of jelly over the inside of the container until the container is evenly coated.

2   Place the container on a flat windowsill. You want the petroleum jelly to be exposed to the air, but protected so that rain won't get inside.

One week

3   Leave the container there for one week.
Tip: most good experiments take time!

4   Look at the inside of your jar. Take a picture. What is all that stuff stuck in the jelly? You're looking at airborne particulates! These could be seeds, pollen, small insects, dust, or other pollutants.

If you want to continue experimenting, wait a month and take another picture to compare with the first one. You can also try putting containers in different areas outside to see how the air quality changes from place to place.

CHAPTER 3

FOOD INSPIRATION
Grow Your Own

The Trouble Down Here

What's your favorite food? Maybe it's pizza, or hot and sour soup. A hamburger with all the fixings? A heaping plate of butter chicken? (Is your tummy rumbling yet?) Food is the fuel that keeps our bodies going, but it also makes us happy. We love how it tastes, we love trading lunch snacks with friends at school, and we love sharing food with family. Ask an astronaut about the things they miss when they're in space, and family dinners or favorite foods will be near the top of the list.

But the happiness we feel when we put food on our tables and in our stomachs is hiding some unpleasant truths. One issue is that not everyone has access to enough food. Another is that the way we grow and produce our food can have severe consequences when it comes to living sustainably on this planet. There are plenty of items on the menu to help us feed ourselves in a healthier way (for us and for the planet), but first it's important to understand the problems.

A Vicious Cycle

Access to food should *not* be a problem. The world produces more than enough to feed everyone on the planet—and in fact, in some regions, food is so plentiful that obesity and overweight are key health concerns. The problem is that food production isn't happening equitably. More than 820 million people don't have enough to eat, often because of poor growing conditions where they live. To help get food to those who need it, areas that can produce food produce more of it. And they do this by gearing up what's known as industrial agriculture.

About one-third of the food that is produced to feed people (not animals) each year ends up being wasted or lost. That food weighs roughly 1.2 trillion kilograms (1.3 billion tons) and would be enough to feed 3 billion people.

Here's where things start to go wrong. Industrial agriculture (food production on a large scale) is anything but "green." In fact, it's one of the least sustainable practices on the planet. The global food system is responsible for one-third of our greenhouse gas emissions. It depends on fossil fuels for transportation and uses harmful chemical fertilizers and pesticides—which can lead to deforestation and water pollution. Can you say "climate change contributor"? It's no surprise that the World Wildlife Fund has called the agricultural industry one of the biggest threats to the environment.

Take the demand for food in certain regions and add it to an increase in unsustainable food production practices, and what do you have? The beginnings of a vicious cycle. People need food, so we produce more food. But the foods we produce (see the "Food Footprints" sidebar) and the way we produce them actually contribute to the climate change that is making certain areas unsuitable for food growth. And around and around it goes.

To top it all off, our population is still growing. By 2050, there could be 9.8 billion people on the planet, which is only going to increase the need for food. Some experts think demand will be at least 60 percent higher in 2050 than it is today. And that means more stress on food supplies, especially in areas that are already struggling to feed their populations.

Food Footprints

You've probably heard of carbon footprints. They measure the greenhouse gases that are emitted as a result of the things we do, such as flying somewhere for a vacation, driving a car, or making something—say, a personal computer or T-shirt. Foods have carbon footprints, too, and some of them are pretty big. Meat and dairy, for example, have the highest carbon footprints. This is partly because livestock produce a lot of methane (by, um, farting), but it's also because it takes a lot of energy to produce the food that comes from those animals, and a lot of energy to grow the food that feeds them. If more people ate less meat, or gave it up entirely, it would have a big impact on the planet. One person switching to a vegetarian diet for a year saves the same amount of emissions as parking the family car for six months.

Feeling Insecure?

If you're not able to get enough safe and nutritious food to help you grow and develop and lead an active and healthy life, you are what's called "food insecure." Sometimes food insecurity happens because food just isn't available, but sometimes it's because a family doesn't have the resources to buy or grow the food they need.

Food insecurity is on the rise, especially in sub-Saharan Africa (where 26.2 percent of the population is hungry); the Caribbean (16.1 percent); and Southern Asia (15.8 percent). Climate change, urbanization, and worsening soil conditions have all contributed to the problem, as have water shortages, pollution, and inequality.

Food insecurity is about more than just grumbling stomachs. Undernourishment can contribute to disease, poor general health, and increased levels of stress. It can also lead to fatigue and a lack of focus, which can make it difficult to concentrate in school or at work. School attendance can be affected, too, with food-insecure kids sometimes needing to get a job and help at home rather than focus on their education.

Drought conditions challenge spring crops.

During the COVID-19 pandemic, families around the world got to experience some food insecurity firsthand. As more and more people got sick, food producers experienced labor shortages. As countries closed their borders to traffic, it became difficult to transport food from where it was made or grown to where it was sold. And panic buying—remember the Great Toilet Paper Shortage of 2020?—made things even worse. Empty shelves and "temporarily unavailable" signs were common at grocery stores. For many of us, this was more of an inconvenience than a dangerous situation, but the pandemic made it a little easier to imagine what true food insecurity looks like.

Deserts and Swamps

A lot of attention is paid to food insecurity in low-income countries, but it's a problem that exists everywhere. People who live in big cities and small towns alike can struggle to put food—especially healthy food—on the table.

"Food deserts" are communities where you have to walk more than 20 minutes to find healthy food, like fresh fruits and veggies. Making matters worse, food deserts are often found in low-income neighborhoods, where many people don't own a car. This makes it even harder to get to a store where healthy food is sold.

A "food swamp" may sound like a good thing (swamped with food—how can that be bad?), but it's not. These are places where unhealthy food choices outnumber, or "swamp," the healthy food choices. It may be difficult to find a supermarket in a food swamp, but you'll probably have lots of choices when it comes to fast-food restaurants or convenience stores that sell highly processed foods like soda, potato chips, and frozen meals.

Food shortages. Food waste. Unsustainable food production. There's a lot going on when it comes to the ways we feed ourselves—and all of it needs a rethink if we want to make sure everyone has enough to eat and the planet thrives. It's time to cook up a new recipe—and astronauts can help.

663 MILLION people around the world are undernourished, meaning they don't get enough food to meet the number of calories or amount of energy they need.

9 PERCENT OF THE GLOBAL POPULATION (about 700 million people) is considered "severely" food insecure, while 25 percent (about 2 billion) is "moderately or severely" food insecure.

40 PERCENT OF THE WORLD'S LANDMASS is arid—meaning it's too dry to grow food. Rising temperatures over the coming years will only make this worse.

THE AMOUNT OF FOOD WE'RE GROWING TODAY will feed just half of the global population by 2050.

FOOD PRODUCTION TAKES A LOT OF WATER—about 1,500 liters (400 gallons) to produce 1 kilogram (2.2 pounds) of wheat, and about 16,000 liters (4,250 gallons) to produce 1 kilogram (2.2 pounds) of beef. As we learned in chapter 1, water is already scarce; by 2050, we'll need twice as much water to produce our food.

Look Up for Inspiration

Astronauts have their own challenges with food. With no fields to sow or crops to harvest, you could say that food insecurity is an even bigger problem in space than it is on Earth. There needs to be enough of the stuff to last the whole mission (or at least until a resupply spacecraft arrives), and it can't take up a ton of room, because there isn't much room to be had. Also, the term "environmental concerns" takes on a new meaning when a floating crumb from a slice of bread or a potato chip can damage highly sensitive and very expensive equipment!

In the early days of the space program, no one was sure how well astronauts would be able to eat and digest food in space. Would they be able to swallow in microgravity? The first astronaut to find out was American John Glenn, during the Mercury mission in 1962. The tubes of pureed beef and vegetables, applesauce, and xylose sugar tablets he "ate," all washed down with water, may not have been the tastiest, but they did provide the calories and nutrition he needed. (They were also easier to store and digest than whole foods.)

Today's astronauts have it better. They can choose from more than 200 food items, most of which, like the food people take on camping trips, need to be rehydrated before eating. Feel like scrambled eggs? Coming right up! Oatmeal, granola, and chicken are also on the menu. Although the risk of floating crumbs still means bread is a no-no, tortillas are a substitute. And you can definitely make a peanut butter and jelly sandwich on one of those!

For now, this system works—at least if you don't mind skipping potato chips for a couple of months. But what happens in the future? With plans underway for longer stays in space, figuring out what to eat is more important than ever.

Astronauts are used to making do with instant coffee. But in November 2014, Italian astronaut Samantha Cristoforetti became the world's first orbiting barista, boldly brewing where no one had brewed before. Latte or espresso, anyone?

Just Add Water, or Air

One way to expand the food choices available to astronauts on missions is to have them grow their own. Over the past two decades, space agencies have been experimenting with growing plants hydroponically or aeroponically in micro-gravity. Hydroponics uses a special liquid solution to deliver nutrients to plant roots. Aeroponics delivers dissolved nutrients to a plant's roots through misty air or small water droplets. Both growing methods are soil-free and reduce water consumption. They also encourage fast growth, which is good if you need a constant supply of food and there are no grocery stores in sight! Space agencies are exploring both methods for use in future lunar missions.

DR. DAVE'S LIFE ON THE ISS

Social Supper

Astronauts may not enjoy a huge variety of food on the ISS, but we still love eating together. In space, dinner is never just a meal; it's a social event that lasts for most of the evening, with each astronaut trying to find something unique to share with others from different crews. One of my favorite spaceflight moments was when the STS-118 shuttle crew got together with the Expedition 15 crew in the Russian segment of the ISS for an evening of great food, friendship, and fun. Just like at a dinner party with friends on Earth, each crew brought food and drinks from their own pantry to share. It was fun tasting some of the cosmonauts' favorite foods, and the ISS crew appreciated having some of the snacks and fresh fruit from the shuttle crew.

Pass the Veggies

In space, veggies aren't just those things we need for a balanced diet. On the ISS, Veggie—short for Vegetable Production System—is actually a garden. Launched in 2014 and about the size of a piece of luggage, Veggie holds six plants. Each grows in a "pillow" filled with a clay-based growth medium and fertilizer that helps to distribute water, nutrients, and air around the roots. This growth medium is important because of the way fluids typically behave in space: without it, the roots could either drown in a big blob of water or gradually end up surrounded by nothing but air.

With no sunlight available, a bank of light-emitting diodes (LEDs) helps the plants to grow. Since plants reflect a lot of green light and use more red and blue wavelengths to help them grow, the Veggie chamber on the ISS usually glows a magenta pink.

Like so many of us, astronauts enjoy caring for their growing plants—particularly when they get to eat the fruits of their labor. Veggie has successfully grown three types of lettuce, Chinese cabbage, mizuna mustard, red Russian kale, and even zinnia flowers. The flowers were especially popular with astronaut Scott Kelly, who in 2016 picked a bouquet and photographed it floating in the cupola against the backdrop of Earth. In 2015, astronauts proudly shared their homegrown produce with their Russian crewmates. NASA astronaut Kjell Lindgren enjoyed adding the lettuce they had grown to his space cheeseburger.

Half of the plants were harvested and eaten by the crew members, with remaining samples returned to Earth to be analyzed. Researchers were concerned that potentially harmful microbes might grow on the produce. So far, no harmful contamination has been detected, and the food has been safe (and enjoyable) for the crew to eat. The food team at the Kennedy Space Center wants to plant more produce in the future, including tomatoes and peppers. Foods like berries and certain beans would be useful as well, since they might provide some protection from space radiation for crew members who eat them. Researchers found that an antioxidant-rich diet, including plenty of green vegetables such as spinach, as well as beetroot and tomatoes, showed promise in reducing the harmful effects of radiation.

Farming in Space?

Like Veggie, the Advanced Plant Habitat, or APH, is a space station growth chamber for plant research. It also uses LED lights and a clay-based growth medium to deliver water, nutrients, and oxygen to the plant roots. But unlike Veggie, it is enclosed and fully automated. As much fun as astronauts have looking after plants, the work can be time-consuming and can take them away from other research and experiments. The APH does the plant-tending all on its own, using cameras and more than 180 sensors that are in constant contact with a team on the ground at the Kennedy Space Center. It also has more colors of LED lights than Veggie, with red, green, and blue lights, but also white, far-red, and even infrared to allow for nighttime imaging.

The APH is the next step on the path to developing self-operating greenhouses that could be used to grow larger numbers of plants on the moon or Mars.

Don Pettit and the Space Zucchini

During their stays on the International Space Station, astronauts are always busy with scientific research. In 2011 and 2012, astronaut Don Pettit was exploring the effects of microgravity on plant growth. Using an aeroponic system—in this case, a zippered plastic bag with just the tiniest bit of water—Pettit grew sunflowers, broccoli, and zucchini. He was so pleased with the results that he named his plants and even started a blog: *The Diary of a Space Zucchini.*

As well as providing a bit of extra food, the growing plants made the space station feel more like home. "There is nothing like the smell of living green in this forest of engineered machinery," Pettit wrote. (If you want to check out a plant's perspective on living in space, enter the words "Don Pettit space zucchini" into an Internet search engine.)

Space on Earth

Veggie and the Advanced Plant Habitat may be cutting-edge tech, but the hydroponic and aeroponic systems they use aren't new. In fact, some experts believe that the Hanging Gardens of Babylon—dating from earlier than 500 BCE and considered one of the Seven Wonders of the Ancient World—were created using a complicated hydroponic system. In a food-insecure world, it may be time for these ancient technologies to make a comeback. Since neither system depends on traditional growing conditions, they can be used in places where it has been, or is becoming, difficult to grow food.

No Soil Required

For many years, Nigeria has been one of those places. Drought is common in this African country, as are shipping delays that spoil produce on its way to market. Making matters worse is the slow expansion of the Sahara Desert, which is gobbling up land that used to be suitable for farming. As if that wasn't bad enough, in 2016 the country's farmers came face-to-face with the *Tuta absoluta* moth. Better known as the tomato leafminer (nickname: "tomato Ebola"), the pest destroyed crops on hundreds of tomato farms. The price of this popular cooking ingredient shot up by 400 percent, making it unaffordable for many Nigerians.

Faced with problem after problem when it came to putting food on the table, people got creative. Not too far from the capital city of Lagos, a fish farmer named Alhaji Bello looked at the wastewater from his fishpond and thought "hydroponics." With help from an organization that is training farmers to use the technology, Bello set up his system. First, bacteria break down the fish poop in the wastewater into nutrients. Then those nutrients are used to feed vegetable plants. Finally, the now-clean water is returned to the fishpond.

A Sustainability Superstar

Yes, it needs water to work, but hydroponic farming is far from being a water hog. In fact, it's extremely water wise. The technique sucks up just 10 percent of the water used by traditional farming methods. That's pretty impressive, but what makes hydroponics a true sustainability superstar is that even the small amount of water it needs can be used again and again. If you happen to live in an area where water is scarce, this is very good news.

Around 6,000 kilometers (3,700 miles) south of Nigeria, Zimbabwe is experiencing its worst drought in more than a century. And because of the country's very old sewage system, what little water there is often isn't safe. As people, grocery stores, and restaurants struggle to keep food available and affordable, hydroponics is becoming more popular. In the city of Harare, for example, a 50-year-old woman named Venensia Mukarati set up a system to grow produce for her family. It worked so well that she started supplying nearby restaurants with lettuce, cucumbers, spinach, and herbs. She's now expanding her greenhouse and is training others to set up their own systems.

No water? No problem!

And it works! In his 8 x 10 meter (26 x 33 foot) "garden"—with no soil in sight—Bello grows more tomatoes, lettuce, and peppers than a traditional garden would. "In soil, a tomato plant produces up to 10 kilograms [22 pounds] of fruit," he says, "whereas with hydroponics, it yields up to 50 kilograms [110 pounds]." And it does this while using fewer resources, protecting plants from weeds and pests, and kicking pesticides to the curb (no soil = no soil-borne diseases).

Bello is one of Nigeria's new "agripreneurs"—a growing group of men and women who are learning how to farm with hydroponics. Knowing that the country's problems with traditional agriculture are likely to get worse, the company that helped train Bello is hoping to train 100,000 more farmers before 2025. Even universities are getting in on the action by offering hydroponics courses as an area of study.

A Big-City Solution

Hydroponic systems are helpful in places where growing conditions aren't ideal because of drought or poor soil. But remember those food deserts and swamps we talked about back on pages 52–53? Well, hydroponics can help there, too.

Hydroponic systems are perfect for spaces like balconies, rooftops, and warehouses. This makes them useful in cities where room to grow food in the traditional way can't be found, and yet food security is still a problem. In Michigan, Kimberly Buffington started PLANTeD, a hydroponic farm that grows food for local restaurants, universities, hospitals—and a neighborhood where food scarcity is a problem. This "urban farmer" is especially proud of growing herbs and veggies that would normally have to be shipped in from California and Mexico.

In New York and Chicago, where some neighborhoods also experience food scarcity, a company called Gotham Greens has set up rooftop greenhouses that grow fresh veggies year-round. Their produce—which includes several types of lettuce as well as herbs—can be found at local grocery stores and online. But Gotham Greens also works with local communities. In Chicago, for example, they provide greens to nonprofits such as the Urban Growers Collective. The collective's Fresh Moves Mobile Market then brings those healthy veggies to schools and community health centers.

Organizations like PLANTeD and Gotham Greens are onto something big: one study found that if cities around the world got in on the act, urban agriculture could produce 200 million tons of food a year. In a world where climate change is making traditional farming methods harder and harder to sustain, that's welcome news.

Hydroponics North

We spend a lot of time worrying about the effects of a warming planet on food production, but what about places where weather conditions are just too cold to grow much of anything? This is a problem in Canada's Far North. In the territory of Nunavut, for example, where fresh fruits and vegetables have to be shipped in from farther south, food insecurity affects 46 percent of the population. A head of broccoli there can cost almost $10, and a bag of grapes $22.

Over the last 100 years, the Sahara Desert has grown by more than 7,600 square kilometers (2,950 square miles) each year. It's now 10 percent bigger than it was in 1920.

Hydroponic grown rice

More Work to Do

Hydroponics and aeroponics can certainly help when it comes to feeding our growing population in a sustainable way, but they aren't perfect solutions.

Right now, the foods that are typically grown in hydroponic farms—mostly low-calorie veggies—are not nutritional powerhouses. On their own, they can't meet all of the needs of a hungry population. To do that, we'd need to figure out how to hydroponically grow calorie-rich root crops (beets, potatoes, and onions, for example), grains (wheat, corn, rice), and tree crops (fruits and nuts). Meat and dairy products are also essential.

A hydroponic farm, even a small one, can also be complicated to set up, not to mention expensive. Equipment has to be purchased and assembled, the plants need nutrients, and heat and light have to be provided artificially—which suck up energy while adding to the costs. And if the power happens to go out? Entire crops can be lost.

Can hydroponic farming adapt to the needs of a hungry planet challenged by climate change? Only time will tell.

Naurvik is a hydroponic food production system in Gjoa Haven, Nunavut, located approximately 250 kilometres north of the Arctic Circle. The name *Naurvik* means the *growing place* in Inuktitut and was chosen by the community during consultations about the project.

In Nunavut and other places like it, companies with names like Freight Farms, CropBox, and Growcer are installing vertical hydroponic farms in shipping containers and sending them north. Growcer's farms are small but mighty, growing between 3,000 and 5,000 plants each—produce that can then be sold at farmers' markets and restaurants for much lower than the cost of food that's shipped north. The Canadian company, which has containers in northern Canada and in Alaska, insulates its farms against the cold so they work at temperatures as low as –52°C (–62°F). Talk about weatherproof!

A container farm is one solution for cold-weather locations, but some experts would like to see larger vertical gardens in these areas, too. The main challenges? The cost of the units and the cost of the energy to operate them.

Strawberry cultivation in a hydroponic greenhouse

Think Like an Astronaut

For as long as astronauts have been in space, they've been learning how to feed themselves in more efficient and sustainable ways—including growing some of their own food. And while that's certainly one way we can think like an astronaut and support sustainable food practices, there are others, too.

Plant a Garden

You don't need a lot of room for a garden. A small space in the backyard or a container on a balcony can get you started. Check online or at a local garden center to find out what grows well in your area. If you want to try growing year-round without worrying about the weather, in-home hydroponic systems can help you grow herbs, vegetables, or fruit.

Visit a Farmers' Market

Eating foods that are grown locally is a good way to help reduce greenhouse gas emissions. Learn more about what's grown in your area—and support the people who are growing it—by checking out your local farmers' market. The produce is fresh and in season, and it doesn't have to be shipped as far before it gets to your table.

Eat More Plants

Earlier, we learned that the production of certain types of food—including meat—comes with a high carbon footprint. Why not put more vegetables, fruits, and plant-based food choices like chickpeas, lentils, and beans on your plate? A balanced diet of sustainable foods helps us to have a healthy body and planet, and to create a sustainable, healthy future.

Consider the Community

Community gardens are on the rise! Found in most North American cities, these are places where people come together to plant and grow food. Sometimes the gardeners keep the produce themselves, and sometimes it is donated to those in need. Does your neighborhood have a community garden? If not, maybe you can talk to a parent, teacher, coach, or community leader about starting one.

Donate to a Food Bank

And one last idea, inspired by Dr. Dave's memories of meals in space: share! If you're fortunate to have enough food on your table every day, why not lend a hand to someone who isn't? Every year, hundreds of thousands of families rely on food banks for a balanced diet. This might change in the future—as projects like the ones we just read about take off—but until then, lots of people still need help. Learn about the food banks in your area and consider making a donation. We all win when we share.

Students, parents, and teachers work in the garden at the 24th Street School on Big Sunday in West Adams, Los Angeles.

Hydroponics at Home

Remember Don Pettit and his space zucchini? In this experiment, you're going to use his method to grow seeds at home. This is a good experiment to try in the spring so that the plants can be put in the soil afterward.

To start, you'll need:

- **a resealable plastic freezer bag**
- **a paper towel**
- **a paper napkin or newspaper**
- **some seeds (you can try zucchini, too, or tomato seeds)**
- **tape**
- **a little water**

1  Tear off a piece of paper towel and trim it if necessary. You need to be able to fold it in half and easily slide it into your plastic freezer bag.

2  Evenly dampen the paper towel so that it is moist. You don't want water everywhere—moist is enough!

3 Lay the paper towel on a flat, clean surface (a plastic food-cutting board works well). Spread a few of your seeds evenly over half of the paper towel.

4  Fold the half of the paper towel with no seeds over the half with the seeds. Gently press the two halves together so the seeds are trapped between the two moist halves.

5  Lay the sandwich bag on the counter beside the paper towel. Carefully slide the paper towel into the bag lying flat on its side. Try not to disturb the seeds. Once the paper towel is inside the bag, use your fingers to gently push the air out of the bag and seal it.

6  Label and date your bag and then tape it to a glass window. You should be able to see the seeds trapped between the two layers of moist paper towel inside the bag.

7  Check on your seedlings every da. If your seeds came from a package, it will tell you when to expect them to "germinate," or sprout. Once they sprout, you can transplant them to some soil in a small pot.

CHAPTER 4

WASTE INSPIRATION
Reduce and Reuse

The Trouble Down Here

You've probably heard of the Great Pacific Garbage Patch, maybe from a teacher, or in something you read on the Internet. There are lots of myths about this giant collection of trash that floats around on the surface of the Pacific Ocean—including that it can be seen from space. Well, that's not true, and neither are the reports that say the patch is the size of Texas (no one really knows how big it is, because it's changing all the time). What *is* true is that it's a mess, and one that we made.

How many things do you throw out in a day? An empty juice box? The wrapper from the granola bar in your lunch? Maybe an empty tube of toothpaste? What about your family and the stuff they're adding to your trash and recycling bins? Now, think of your school, and the arena where you play sports, and the store where your family buys groceries. Each one of those places produces a whole bunch of waste every single day. No wonder Earth has a huge problem with trash!

Too Much of the Wrong Thing

It wasn't always this way, even though humans have always made garbage. Thousands of years ago, we left bones and shells and uneaten food next to cooking fires, or created early versions of dumps just outside of settlements. But the kind of trash our ancestors produced was biodegradable; left alone for long enough, it would break down and be absorbed back into the soil without doing any harm.

These days, our garbage isn't so eco-friendly. Paint, batteries, tires, and other hazardous materials often find their way into the garbage pile, even though they are toxic and should be disposed of properly. "E-waste" is created when we throw away old smartphones, tablets, and computers. And then there's plastic. We make *a lot* of things out of the stuff, and package even more things in it. Rip the packaging off a new toy (probably made of plastic) and where does it go? Straight into the trash or recycling bin. And what about the toy itself, once it breaks or you've outgrown it? Into the trash as well. A lot of that plastic ends up in landfills, where it sticks around for hundreds of years. Some of it also releases chemicals as it breaks down.

In the United States in 2018, 500 million plastic straws were used every day. If you'd placed those end to end, the line would have been long enough to circle Earth twice. Thankfully, some towns, cities, states, and provinces have now banned the use of plastic straws.

The other problem is that there are more of us than ever before. In 2016, the world's population was 7.43 billion—and all of those people produced a whopping 2.01 trillion kilograms (4.43 trillion pounds) of garbage. Can't picture it? Try imagining the Empire State Building. Now, multiply that by 7,000. Seven thousand Empire State Buildings' worth of trash. And the population just keeps growing. In 2022, there were roughly 7.8 billion people on Earth. By 2050, that number is expected to hit 9.7 billion. Just imagine the piles of garbage all those people will make.

One Big Mess

All of that trash creates problems—not one big mess, really, but lots of messes, in lots of different places. Our oceans are filling up with plastic, threatening marine life and the people who depend on the ocean for work. Landfills are big emitters of methane gas and CO_2, which contribute to climate change. And in countries where garbage collection isn't properly managed, the buildup can lead to sickness, disease, and pollution.

Making things worse is that some of the world's biggest producers of trash—countries such as the United States, Canada, and the United Kingdom—pack up their garbage and send it off to poorer countries for recycling. While this sounds like a good idea for creating jobs, there's plenty of room for corruption. Too often, that waste ends up burned or dumped into landfills instead of recycled, releasing chemicals and toxins in a town or city

What Kind of Waste?

In this chapter, we're focusing on the kind of waste people throw into garbage cans, recycling bins, or organic waste containers. We're talking plastic, cardboard, aluminum, food waste, old furniture and clothes, video games that don't work in the new video game system. You get the idea. (And hopefully, you don't throw all of that away! See pages 83 and 84 for more ideas about that.) To learn more about how human waste can also be a problem on Earth and in space, check out chapter 1.

that didn't even create the garbage in the first place.

"But I Recycle!"

"But wait," you're probably saying. "I recycle!" That's a good thing—recycling is an important part of any waste management program—but it can't be the only thing we do. One reason is that we're not recycling enough. While many people believe that recycling is a key way to live more sustainably, the truth is that a bunch more aren't on board. With a recycling rate of 35 percent, the United States is in the middle of the pack. Germany leads at 66 percent, while Saint Lucia, Monaco, and Azerbaijan are among several countries with a rate of 0 percent. With stats like that, it's no wonder so much garbage skips the recycling plant and ends up in landfills.

There are other problems, too. Sometimes, things that shouldn't be recycled end up in our bins. A bit of yogurt or peanut butter left in the bottom of a container may seem harmless, but it has the power to contaminate a ton of paper on its way to a recycling plant, sending it to the dump instead. And then, there's the way our efforts can create a false sense of accomplishment. While we're busy patting ourselves on the back for recycling our plastics and cardboard and glass, we can too easily forget the bigger problem: that our consumer habits just aren't sustainable.

Only 9 percent of the plastic created since the 1950s has been recycled.

BREAKING IT DOWN

Earth's relationship with trash is complicated—it would take a book much longer than this one to explain exactly how we got into this giant mess. But the whole thing can be summed up pretty easily: there are too many people throwing away too many things. For the sake of the planet and everything that lives on it, we need to figure out a better way to reduce and manage our trash.

THE UNITED STATES IS tops when it comes to trash—but not in a good way. Each person in the U.S. produces 730 kilograms (1,609 pounds) of garbage every year. That means a country with just 4 percent of the world's people throws out 12 percent of the world's waste.

FOR EVERY $10 that we spend on buying things, $1 goes toward the packaging. Add that packaging up, and it equals 65 percent of household trash. About one-third of the space in an average dump is filled with packaging.

IT COSTS MONEY TO DEAL WITH OUR TRASH: $30 per ton to recycle, $50 to send it to a landfill, and $65 to $75 to burn it.

IN 2020, the world tossed out 59 million tons of e-waste. That's about the same weight as 350 cruise ships.

AT LEAST 2 BILLION people around the world do not have their trash collected regularly, causing it to build up near where they live.

Look Up for Inspiration

When it comes to trash, the ISS and Earth have a lot in common. Just like us, astronauts produce too much of it. And also just like us, space agencies are looking for ways to reduce and reuse, especially as they plan for journeys that will take astronauts farther away from Earth for longer stays.

Resupply missions deliver about 20,000 kilograms (44,000 pounds) of food, equipment, clothing, cards, and letter to the ISS each year.

Taking Out the Trash

The International Space Station isn't a big place. At about 109 meters (356 feet) long and 73 meters (239 feet) wide, it's roughly the size of a soccer field. Two-thirds of that space is taken up with equipment and storage, leaving just one-third as room for up to seven astronauts. In such tight quarters, garbage can quickly pile up. In fact, up to 2,000 kilograms (4,400 pounds) of trash may have to be stored on board.

When it's time to "take out the trash," the astronauts squish it into trash bags, kind of like we do. But instead of taking those bags to a trash can, they wait until a resupply spacecraft arrives. Once its cargo is unloaded, the spacecraft is loaded up again—this time with ISS garbage. All of those bags either are burned up during re-entry to Earth's atmosphere or return to Earth with the spacecraft.

It's not even close to a sustainable system. Burning up the trash creates environmental problems, and bringing it back to Earth just means someone else has to deal with it. And it only works because the ISS is close enough to Earth for a resupply ship to function as a garbage truck. What will happen when the next moon mission is launched? Or a future mission to Mars? Storing trash on board a small interplanetary spacecraft won't work. There will likely be even less space there than on the ISS, and having lots of trash around would be a health hazard. And a lunar landfill is not an option, either. Who wants to pollute another environment? With all of this in mind, finding a sustainable way to take out the trash in space is a priority.

DR. DAVE'S LIVING IN SPACE

Choose the Grapes!

As I was getting ready for my first mission—a 16-day spaceflight that would feature a lot of neuroscience research—I learned just how important it is to both think about trash and manage it well. Astronauts love having fresh fruit and vegetables to eat during the first few days of a mission. Oranges and bananas seemed like a great choice. That is until our commander reminded us that any trash we created would have to be stored and brought back with us. It didn't take us long to realize that the smell of 16-day-old banana peels and orange rinds is . . . well . . . gross. Turns out grapes—which can be completely eaten—were a much better choice!

Turning Up the Heat

To get the job done, space agencies are working on a two-step approach. Step one is to reduce the amount of trash created by making sure almost everything is recycled or reused. Step two is to develop new technologies to safely dispose of what can't be recycled. One of those new technologies is NASA's Heat Melt Compactor (HMC).

Fruit and goodies are unpacked by Expedition 61 crewmembers (from left) Jessica Meir, Andrew Morgan, Christina Koch, and Luca Parmitano.

The HMC starts by compacting trash into 23-centimeter (9-inch) square "tiles" (about one-eighth of the volume of the original trash). Those tiles are then heated to 150°C (302°F). This sterilizes the material, boils off any water that happens to be sticking around, and gets rid of harmful gases. The water is recovered for use on board. The gases are either released into space or converted into gases that are safe for the space station air system. And the trash tiles? They are now ready to use as radiation shielding. Talk about recycling and reusing!

The Heat Melt Compactor (HMC), a potential trash management system for future, long-duration space missions

Trash to Gas

Another option for trash disposal is OSCAR. No, not the green, garbage-loving grouch from *Sesame Street*, but the Orbital Syngas/Commodity Augmentation Reactor (OSCAR is *much* easier to remember!). This nifty new technology features a reactor that uses heat, oxygen, and steam to turn all sorts of space trash into water and gas. The "syngas" (or synthetic gas) created during this process includes carbon dioxide, carbon monoxide, water vapor, and methane. The hope is that syngas might one day be used as fuel.

In December 2019, OSCAR moved out of the lab and into space for a test on board Blue Origin's *New Shepard* rocket. On this sub-orbital flight (meaning the rocket reached space but did not go into orbit like the space

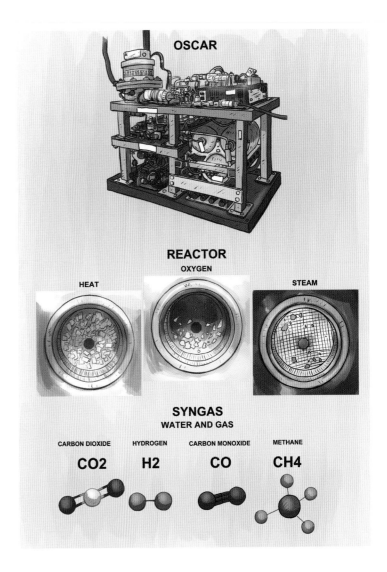

station), OSCAR got the job done and successfully converted trash to gas. For the team of NASA researchers working on the technology, this was excellent news. They've calculated that a four-person, one-year mission to, say, the moon, will produce more than 2,600 kilograms (5,700 pounds) of waste.

"We call it logistical waste," says Annie Meier, who manages the OSCAR research team. "It includes hygiene items like wipes, tooth-paste, and bristles on a toothbrush, food packing, and even clothing because astronauts don't have a washing machine."

While Meier and her team are focused on getting OSCAR into space, she also thinks it might be helpful on Earth, in places like hospitals, cafeterias, and isolated communities. "Hopefully, the things that we learn can help improve waste energy technology and make it more efficient."

Junk in Space

Figuring out how to take out the trash on the ISS or other spacecraft is definitely important for the future of space travel. But managing trash sustainably in space means looking beyond the walls of our spacecraft, too.

Given the mess humans have made on Earth, it's probably not too surprising to learn that we've been messing up space as well. Since the 1950s, when we first started to explore the skies above us, space agencies have launched thousands of rockets and satellites. Right now, there are about 2,000 active satellites orbiting Earth. But there are also about 3,000 "dead" ones up there—satellites that either have completed their missions or no longer work.

And these big pieces of "space junk" have company. According to NASA, there are 23,000 pieces of debris larger than the size of a softball orbiting Earth. There are also 500,000 pieces the size of a marble or larger, and more than 100 million pieces of super-small debris (less than 1 millimeter, or 0.04 inches).

What is all of this stuff? It might be tiny flecks of paint that fall off of rockets when they reach space. Or it could be small pieces of material left over when satellites are destroyed by space agencies or collide with other objects. But no matter where it comes from, space junk is a problem. It can damage working satellites, affecting research in space and communication systems on Earth. And it can also be dangerous. In November 2021, the ISS had to change position by 1.2 kilometers (0.7 miles) to avoid a piece of space junk that flashed by about a mile away, moving at a speed of about 28,200 kilometers (17,500 miles) per hour. A collision could have caused damage to the space station and put astronauts at risk.

Companies around the world are looking for ways to clean up space junk. In Japan, Astroscale is testing the use of magnets to attract space debris. And a partnership between a Swiss company called ClearSpace and the European Space Agency plans to send a trash-collecting spacecraft into orbit in 2025.

What's Up There?

The moon's surface is full of things left by space missions, including:

- moon buggies from Apollo 15, 16, and 17
- 54 probes
- flags
- photos
- an aluminum sculpture called *Fallen Astronaut*
- golf balls
- garbage (like wipes and food packaging)
- human waste
- the ashes of Gene Shoemaker, a U.S. geologist who discovered many comets and planets

Space on Earth

Like the astronauts on the ISS and the space agencies that support them, many people on Earth are experimenting with more sustainable ways to deal with trash. The three Rs—reduce, reuse, and recycle—are all part of the plan.

Cleaning Up with Compactors

One way to reduce our trash is to make it as small as possible (like the first step in the Heat Melt Compactor process we explored on page 75). Around the world, trash compactors are doing just that—making smaller piles of waste out of the big piles that end up in our trash cans and landfills.

In London, U.K., for example, a local deli recently started using two compactors: one for cardboard and one for other waste. Thanks to the compactors, they were able to get rid of three of their big garbage bins. This freed up much-needed space for storage and also cut down on the volume of the garbage they had to get rid of. And in Collier County, Florida, 24 solar-powered trash compactors were installed on beaches and in marinas. The number-one benefit is that these compactors can hold five times as much garbage as an ordinary trash can, which means beaches and public areas stay cleaner for longer. But coming in a close second is that the fully enclosed units keep waste away from wildlife.

While compactors definitely help cut down on the space that trash takes up, they don't help reduce the amount of trash itself. And that's a problem that needs to be solved if we don't want to dump our garbage on future generations.

Looking for Energy at the Landfill

On page 75, we learned how space agencies are exploring trash-to-gas technology to help manage waste on the International Space Station and beyond. That's happening on Earth, too.

In Montreal, for example, the Biomont Energie plant sits close to a former landfill site. A public park now hides the piles of trash that used to be visible here, but under the grass and trees, the garbage itself is still decomposing—and that creates methane emissions. Biomont uses pods placed around the site to collect those emissions. The methane is transferred to the plant, where it is filtered and then burned to create electricity. The process also creates a lot of heat, but even that is put to use. The hot air is used to warm water, which is then pumped out of the

Recycled Roadways

In 1999, lightning struck a hillside near Westley, California, starting a fire that ripped through the 7 million scrap tires piled there. Fumes, soot, and toxic chemicals billowed into the air for five weeks as firefighters fought to get the blaze under control. The fire—and others like it—made it clear that having so many tires in dumps was a huge safety hazard.

One solution to this problem could be hiding in plain sight. In the United States, the Federal Highway Administration has been using old tires to help pave roads in a few warm-weather states since the 1960s. Rubberized asphalt is made with a material called "crumb rubber," which is created by recycling 12 million scrap tires each year. Compared to traditional asphalt, the rubberized version lasts longer, uses fewer raw materials, and is environmentally friendly. Repaving just 1.6 kilometers (1 mile) of one lane of a road with rubberized asphalt 5 centimeters (2 inches) thick would use 2,000 scrap tires. The innovation is currently being tested in several colder states and countries, including Switzerland. If it catches on, it could keep a lot of tires out of landfills.

plant and sent to a building across the street—a building that now has a new source of heat and no longer needs to use natural gas. A win-win situation!

Putting Poop to Work

If we can put our landfill sites to work in creating cleaner sources of energy, why not look to other types of trash, too? "Biogas" is created when organic materials (plant and animal products) are allowed to break down in an oxygen-free (anaerobic) environment, producing a renewable energy source. In Salisbury, Vermont, the Goodrich Family Farm is home to the northeastern United States' largest anaerobic digester—which takes cow manure and food waste and turns them into renewable natural gas (RNG). The Goodrich dairy farm's 900 cows provide the manure, and local businesses, including the head office of Ben & Jerry's ice cream, provide the food waste. Each day, the digester is able to recycle 100 tons of poop and 180 tons of food into RNG. The gas is then piped to customers who are willing to pay a little more for a low-carbon source of energy. Nearby Middlebury College buys more than half of the gas produced at the farm. Thanks in part to this new and renewable source of energy, it has been able to stop using fossil fuels to heat its buildings.

Biogas systems have potential. If the United States embraced the technology fully, it could produce enough renewable energy to power 3 million homes.

On the other side of the world, in Nepal, people are also putting poop to good use. In the village of Dalla, Jeet Bhadur Tharu's family used to use up to 7 kilograms (15 pounds) of firewood a day for cooking. The farmer's wife and daughters had to gather

BIOGAS

the wood and cook in the poorly ventilated kitchen (see chapter 2 for more on why this can be a problem). Now, almost all of their cooking is done with cleaner-burning methane—thanks to one of the many biogas projects the government is helping to build.

Behind Tharu's home are a concrete mixing bowl and an outhouse. Dung from his buffalo and cows goes into the mixing bowl, along with water. A metal crank combines the mixture and pushes it into a pipe that leads to an airtight pit underground. The human waste from the outhouse also ends up in the pit, thanks to gravity and water. Once in the pit, the waste breaks down, releasing methane—which is piped into the kitchen, where it's used for cooking.

Nepal's Alternative Energy Promotion Centre has already helped to build 200,000 systems and is aiming to hit the 2 million mark. Biogas projects are also being built in many other countries where air pollution from cooking fires and water pollution from improper waste disposal are concerns.

Garbage Spies in the Skies

Space-age tech is helping us to reduce and reuse our garbage, but it's also pitching in with the messes we've already made. At Plymouth Marine Laboratory in the United Kingdom, marine satellite scientist Lauren Biermann and her colleagues used images from the Sentinel-2A and Sentinel-2B satellites to find patches of plastic waste in the ocean off British Columbia and Scotland. Plastics, it turns out, reflect light differently than natural materials like wood or seaweed, and so they show up differently on the satellite images. While the Sentinel satellites were originally sent into orbit to take pictures of Earth's landforms, they are now a valuable source of information on ocean pollution. The next step? Figuring out where that waste is coming from and taking steps to reduce it.

Think Like an Astronaut

How can you think like an astronaut when it comes to trash? You can start by imagining that you have very little space for trash in your life (because you really do!), and then you can keep the three Rs in mind. Recycling is important, but as we learned on page 71, it can't be the only solution. It's more important to reduce and reuse, if possible. Here are some simple ways you can challenge yourself to do that.

Compost

Think about composting as reusing the parts of your food that you don't eat! Each year, more than 1 billion tons of food get wasted. Some of that is because we buy too much or prepare too much, and don't always eat our leftovers. But it's also because the parts of the food we don't use (for example, some seeds, pits, bones, skin) end up in the garbage instead of the compost bin. If your city or town collects green waste, make sure your household uses a green-waste container in your kitchen. Or consider starting a composting project in your backyard.

Get to Know Your Bins

Should yogurt containers go in the garbage or the recycling bin? What about juice boxes or candy wrappers? If you're confused about what piece of trash should go in what bin, you aren't alone: more than half of Americans admit they aren't sure how to recycle. In this chapter, we learned just how much recycling actually ends up in landfills. You can help your family do better by checking out the rules in your community. Visit your local government's website for more information on what waste goes where.

Give Upcycling a Try

Before dropping something into the trash can or recycling bin, why not take a closer look? It's possible there may be another use for that object. When you take trash and create something new out of it, it's called "upcycling," and there are tons of ways to do it. Tin cans can be cleaned and painted to become pencil holders. Plastic bottles can turn into bird feeders. Old sweaters can be turned into hats or mittens. Search the Internet for "upcycling projects" for tons of good ideas. You'll have fun making something, and it will cut down on your trash.

Donate

If you can't upcycle something that's headed for the trash heap, consider donating it instead. Remember your old T-shirt? The one you really liked but doesn't fit you anymore? If it's still in good condition, consider passing it on to a used clothing drive or a local thrift shop. And don't stop there! You can do the same with sporting equipment you no longer use, games you don't play, or even old electronics. Your trash might just be someone else's treasure.

Zero-Waste Wednesday

You've heard of Meatless Monday and Taco Tuesday, right? Why not give Zero-Waste Wednesday (ZWW) a try? Pick any day of the week and try to live garbage free. That means bringing a no-trash lunch to school, with everything in reusable containers, or buying only lunch items that come on reusable dishes. Eat everything on your plate and drink everything you pour. And stay away from single-use paper and plastic items like straws and napkins. Worried that your one day won't make a difference? Consider that if 1,000 people took on the ZWW challenge, it would reduce the amount of trash produced on that day by 2,000 kilograms (4,400 pounds)! Why not get your friends involved, too?

EXPERIMENTING WITH DR. DAVE

Make an R-Plan

This is more of an activity than an experiment, but it's just as useful! An R-plan is a recycling plan, and if we're really serious about cutting down on waste, we should have one for everything we buy. What happens when we no longer need that shirt or toy or smartphone? Will it be recycled or donated? Or can it be used as something else?

Challenge your friends to use 2 L (0.5 gal.) plastic soda pop bottles and turn them into something new. You could cut one in half, take the cap off, and nest the top half upside down inside the bottom half. Fill the bottom half with a bit of water and the top half with soil, and use it as a self-watering planter for the germinated seeds from our chapter 3 experiment. You could also leave the cap on, turn the upper half upside down, and attach strings to it to make a hanging plant holder. What else can you make?

CHAPTER 5

ENERGY INSPIRATION
Say Goodbye to Fossil Fuels

The Trouble Down Here

We've explored some big challenges in this book. Keeping our water and air clean. Feeding a growing population. Cutting down on trash. They're all important—whether we're talking about living sustainably on this planet or living sustainably in space. Despite how different these challenges may seem on the surface, they all have something in common: a shared connection to our dependence on fossil fuels. For a long time, we didn't realize the damage these fuels were doing to our environment. But we do now, and it's up to us to figure out a better way of powering our world.

Power Problems

There's no doubt about it: humans are addicted to fossil fuels. In the past 100 years—the blink of an eye in the planet's history—we've come to rely on burning fossil fuels in so many ways. They're in the gas we use to drive our cars (and the fuel we use to power rockets); they help provide electricity for our homes and buildings; and they support the manufacturing of almost everything we buy. They are the most important energy source in our world, meeting more than 80 percent of our needs. It's pretty hard to imagine where we'd be without them.

But . . . there's a downside to all of that power—a few downsides, actually.

HIDE AND SEEK

Fossil fuels such as oil, coal, and natural gas aren't just sitting around waiting for us to use them.

Quick refresher: Fossil fuels are made from the decomposing remains of plants and animals. (We're talking *really old* plants and animals, ones that lived millions of years ago.) They hang out in Earth's crust, and getting to them means drilling, mining, or fracking—where water, sand, and chemicals are injected into rock to force open cracks and release the oil or gas inside. Those activities can be harmful to the environment, and some can be dangerous for people, too. In 2021, an explosion at a coal mine in Russia killed 46 miners and 6 rescuers.

DIRTY BUSINESS

Fossil fuels all contain carbon and hydrogen, which can be burned to create energy. That's the good news; it's this energy that powers all of our stuff. But burning fossil fuels is also a dirty business. When they're burned, they release carbon dioxide and other greenhouse gases into the atmosphere. Over the last 20 years, fossil fuels have been responsible for almost 75 percent of the emissions that come from human activity. That makes them the top contributor to global warming and climate change. So the next time you hear about melting ice caps, rising sea levels, floods, or droughts, you'll have a pretty good idea of where the problem started.

Every day, humans consume more than 1 million terajoules of energy. What does that mean? Picture 7.5 billion people each boiling 70 kettles of water an hour, for 24 straight hours.

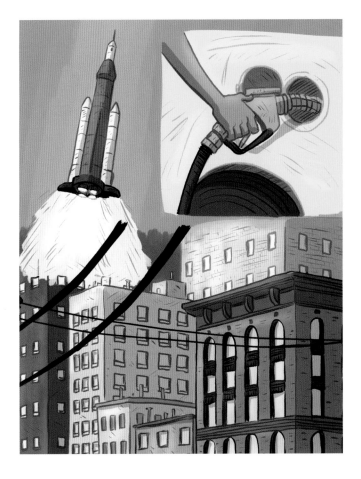

Burning coal is a major contributor to fossil fuel pollution.

NO EQUALITY HERE

Another tricky thing is that fossil fuels aren't evenly located around the world. Some countries, like China and the United States, have lots of coal. Others, like Saudi Arabia and Canada, are rich in oil. Transporting fossil fuels to the places that need them is expensive. It also uses—you guessed it—more fossil fuels and creates more emissions. And if a country that needs, say, oil isn't getting along with the country that has it? Well, that can cause political problems and raise the price we pay for using that fuel.

GOING, GOING, GONE . . .

Hard to get at, dirty, expensive. That's all bad enough. But there's another downside to our fossil fuel addiction. Fossil fuels are a nonrenewable energy source. That means that once they're gone, they're gone. Experts disagree about how long they'll last if we keep using them the way we are now. Some say oil could be gone in 50 years; others say 30. With coal, it's anywhere from 70 to 150 years. The biggest problem of all, though, is that guesses about how long fossil fuels will last are missing the point. If we stay on the same path, it's not just the fossil fuels that will be gone, gone, gone—it's the entire future of our planet and everything that calls it home.

Say Hello to Renewables

If we don't want to say goodbye to life as we know it on this planet, we have to find alternatives to fossil fuels. Renewable energy sources could be part of the solution. Unlike fossil fuels, renewables can't be used up. Here's a quick rundown of the options:

Solar: Solar panels capture the sun's energy and use it for heat, or it can be turned into electricity.

Wind: Turbines harness the power of wind currents and convert it into electricity.

Hydro: Turbines grab the energy of flowing water (through dams, for example, or over waterfalls) and turn it into electricity.

Geothermal: Steam and hot water from Earth's core are used to provide heat or create electricity.

Biomass: Plant and animal matter (like wood, manure, garbage, or food waste) are burned to produce energy or converted into a liquid "biofuel".

"So what's the holdup?" you're probably asking. "Why can't we just switch to these more sustainable energy sources?"

That sounds like a great idea, but it's not so simple. Renewable energy is renewable—which is a huge plus—but it can also be expensive. And it can be difficult to access when and where it's needed. How can you rely on solar power when the sun

Photovoltaic solar panels on the slope above valley in Mount Aspiring National Park, South Island, New Zealand

isn't shining, or wind power on a calm day? There are other questions that need to be answered, too. Is hydro power the answer if dams need to be built, destroying the land around them and forcing people to move? And how are we supposed to store all of the energy produced? Until we're able to make sure that everyone has equal and affordable access to the energy they need, our power problems won't be solved.

Even with the challenges ahead, there's no question that renewable energy is our best hope for a more sustainable future. And once again, we can look up for inspiration on how to get the job done.

An Uphill Battle

We know that it's important to cut back on our use of fossil fuels in order to live more sustainably. But we're facing an uphill battle. Our population continues to grow, which means there will be more of us using energy for all sorts of things. Many countries around the world are also becoming more industrialized and using more energy along the way. And rising global temperatures mean a higher demand for cooling systems for our homes and buildings. Add it all together, and some experts predict that world energy consumption will increase by 50 percent by 2040. For the sake of the planet and everything that lives on it, we need to do something about our fossil fuel addiction—and fast.

**WHEN IT COMES TO CO_2
EMISSIONS,** China is the worst
emitter, with 33 percent of total world
emissions in 2021. The United States is next, with
13 percent. Third place goes to India, with 7 percent.

IN 2019, 33 PERCENT OF THE WORLD'S ENERGY was
supplied by oil, 27 percent by coal, and 24 percent by gas.

21 PERCENT of people around the world do not
have access to electricity.

A SINGLE WIND TURBINE can provide energy to 300 homes.

NORWAY, BRAZIL, AND NEW ZEALAND use more
renewable energy than any other countries. Norway relies
on hydro power for 45 percent of its energy; Brazil
depends on biofuel and waste energy for
32 percent of its supply; and New Zealand
taps into wind and solar power for
25 percent of its energy needs.

Look Up for Inspiration

Fossil fuels are clearly a problem on Earth, but on the International Space Station, they don't exist. No wonder astronauts are a great source of inspiration when it comes to different ways of powering our world.

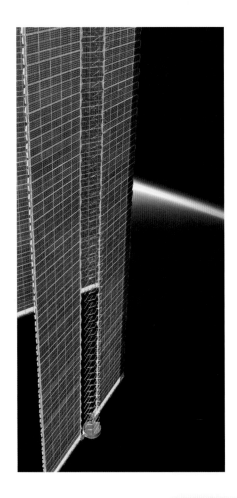

Sun + Battery = Reliable Power

In some ways, the space station is very different from our homes on Earth. But in other ways, it's pretty similar. For instance, most things on the ISS require electricity. Fans are used to circulate the air, and lights are used inside and outside the station. They all need power, as do toilets, computers, control systems, robotic systems, and exercise equipment. But with no power grid to plug into, where does that electricity come from?

Here's a pretty awesome fact: the space station gets *100 percent* of its energy from the sun. How? The ISS has 16 giant solar panels (called arrays)—eight on each side—that stick out from the main truss, which holds the modules where the astronauts live and work. The ISS orbits Earth every 90 minutes, so the position of the solar panels changes to capture as much of the sun's energy as possible. The Solar Alpha Rotary Joint (SARJ) is used to rotate their position.

Over the next several years, six new solar arrays will arrive at the International Space Station aboard three SpaceX cargo spacecraft. They will work with the original solar arrays to increase solar power generation to 215 kilowatts.

The ISS systems and research equipment need a lot of electricity. Thankfully, the solar arrays are up to the job. By capturing the sun's rays, they are able to generate 84 to 120 kilowatts of energy every 45 minutes (during what's called "orbital daytime"). That's enough to power 40 homes. That electricity is transferred to large batteries attached to the truss. By storing the energy harnessed from the sun, these batteries make it possible for the ISS to have power all the time—even when it travels around the far side of Earth, where the sun's rays don't reach. For the 45 minutes it takes for the ISS to get back to the sunlit side of the planet, batteries are the station's only source of electricity.

Turn Down the Heat!

When the source of your electricity is the sun, things are probably going to get warm, right? Actually, most electrically powered things generate heat—regardless of where that electricity comes

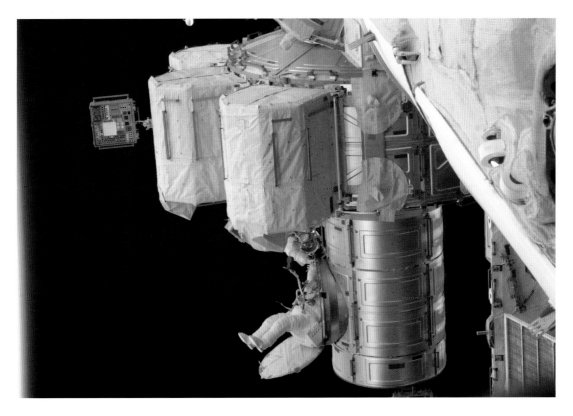

A space walk to switch batteries

Changing the Batteries

All batteries need to be replaced at some point. You've probably done it yourself for a TV remote or a toy. Easy, right? Well, switching batteries on the space station is not so simple. After years of research, planning, and training, it took 14 spacewalks to swap them out. The job of replacing the original nickel-hydrogen batteries with newer lithium-ion batteries began in 2016 and finished in 2020, when the last of the six new batteries was installed. They are expected to last for 10 years.

from. We just don't notice this so much in our homes because we're pretty lucky when it comes to temperature control. First of all, we don't have tons of scientific equipment running in our homes. Second, we can open windows to let in fresh air. We also have furnaces or other sources of heat to warm things up when the temperature outside drops, and insulation to retain that heat. Many homes also have air-conditioning, which makes it comfortable indoors even when it's hot outside.

In space, temperature control isn't so easy. The temperatures outside the ISS soar to 121°C (250°F) on the sun-facing side and sink to –157°C (–250°F) on the dark side. But most humans—astronauts included—prefer to live and work in conditions around 22°C (72°F). The challenge, then, is coming up with a system that captures heat when it's needed and gets rid of it when it's not.

That's where the Active Thermal Control System comes in . . .

The Active Thermal Control System

The Active Thermal Control System, or ATCS, is one smart piece of technology. Working in partnership with space-age insulation, and the conditions that already exist on board the ISS, its sophisticated cooling systems keep the temperature not too hot and not too cold.

INSULATION ON THE JOB

Let's start with the insulation. You've probably seen it before—maybe in your home or at a hardware store. It's that fluffy pink or yellow material that gets stuffed between the inside and outside walls of a building. Its job is to slow the transfer of heat from one area to another (from inside to outside on a cold day, for example, or from outside to inside on a warm one).

Insulation on the space station works in the same way—sort of. A big part of its job is to prevent the heat generated by all of that solar-powered equipment from escaping, and to prevent the extreme cold of space from getting in. But space insulation also needs to protect astronauts from harmful solar radiation. Because of that added job, ISS insulation doesn't look like Earth insulation; it's less like cotton candy and more like a blanket made out of tinfoil. It's called Multi-Layer Insulation and is made of Mylar and a fabric called Dacron. The Mylar layers prevent radiation from getting through, and the Dacron

keeps the Mylar sheets apart, which prevents heat from moving too easily between layers. In fact, it's so good at preventing heat from escaping that sometimes things get a little too warm—which is where the cooling system comes in.

KEEPING IT COOL

To keep the ISS from getting too warm, the Active Thermal Control System takes the heat produced by electrical equipment and transfers it to water-cooled plates. It does this through a process called conduction. Think about what happens when you hold an ice cube in your hand. It melts, right? That's because the heat from your body is transferred—or conducted—into the ice cube. When that happens, your hand is also left feeling colder.

That's what happens on the ISS. The heat from equipment and instruments is conducted into the water-cooled plates. This helps to make sure that the equipment doesn't overheat, but it also makes it possible to get rid of the heat. The water in the cooling plates—now warm—is sent to a heat exchanger. That exchanger transfers the heat again, this time to liquid-ammonia cooling loops that circulate outside the space station to radiator panels (the ammonia prevents the water from freezing). And those panels transfer the heat to the vacuum of space. So long, extra heat!

Power Down!

In 2010 and again in 2013, the ISS experienced cooling system failures. The astronauts were not in any danger either time, but the temperature-regulation system was working at only about half its regular capacity. This meant that some experiments, operations, and equipment had to be powered down to prevent things from getting too hot. The culprits? Malfunctions in the cooling loops.

DR. DAVE'S LIFE ON THE ISS

Dangerous Work

On my first spacewalk, Rick Mastracchio and I installed a new section to the long truss that holds the solar arrays and other equipment in place. I was working very close to one of the solar arrays and had to be careful not to touch the array itself, due to the possibility of electrical shock. A couple of months later, in October 2007, astronauts noticed a 76-centimeter (30-inch) tear in one of the arrays. Astronaut Scott Parazynski performed a spacewalk to successfully repair the tear. It was dangerous work. Before Scott set out on his mission, fellow astronaut Paolo Nespoli went over a list of warnings with him, including all of the things he had to avoid in order to stay safe: sharp edges, the solar cells, hinges that could pinch his suit. About halfway through, Scott interrupted his fellow astronaut: "I'm not sure there's much left to touch," he said. Later, he joked that it was a good thing he hadn't seen any sparks!

Space on Earth

Kicking our addiction to fossil fuels would be a huge step toward living more sustainably—whether we're talking about powering our cars and factories or about heating or cooling our buildings. Around the world, people are getting serious about meeting this goal. Lots of renewable energy projects are in the works, and many feature technologies like those being used on the ISS.

Sun Power

We've known about the power of the sun for a long time—a really long time. As far back as the seventh century BCE, our ancestors used sunlight and magnifying glasses to start fires. Solar power has come a long way since then.

These days, companies such as Target, Amazon, Walmart, and IKEA are investing in solar installations to power their operations. And in 2015, India's Cochin International Airport became the first in the world to run entirely on solar power. By the following year, the airport not only stopped paying for its own electricity but was also contributing to the city's power grid. Even China—the worst emitter of CO_2—is trying to do better. As of 2021, it had the world's largest solar energy capacity, at 306,000 megawatts. By the time you are reading this book, the country will be able to supply solar power at the same cost as coal.

With so many countries trying to lower their CO_2 emissions and switch to cleaner sources of energy, it's no surprise that solar power plants are popping up all over. The world's biggest is the Noor Ouarzazate Solar Complex in Morocco. The plant covers an area of more than 3,000 hectares (7,415 acres) of the Sahara Desert. That's about 3,000 times the size of the sports field at your local high school. The complex has a capacity of 580 megawatts, which is enough to provide electricity to about 1 million people.

If we could capture it all—say, with solar panels—one hour of sunlight could power the whole world for an entire year.

Storage Solutions

Our biggest challenge with renewable energy sources isn't capturing the energy but storing it. Right now, the main option is a lithium-ion battery. But as Bill Gates once wrote, "If you wanted to store enough electricity to run everything in your house for a week, you would need a huge battery—and it would triple your electric bill."

There are other problems with lithium-ion batteries, too. Extracting the raw materials needed to make them (lithium and cobalt) takes a lot of energy, which adds to our CO_2 emissions. And the mines can be unsafe for workers, some of whom are children.

With this in mind, innovators are on the hunt for alternatives. Pumped hydroelectric storage is one option. With this technology—which has been around since the 1920s—excess power is used to pump water up into a reservoir. During times when not as much solar or wind power is produced, the water is released through turbines to generate electricity. Governments in Quebec and Ontario are investing in this technology to expand their use of green energy sources.

Then there's gravity storage. It works like pumped hydroelectric storage, but instead of lifting water to higher ground, the system uses excess power and cables or pullies to lift heavy objects, like rocks or bricks. When power is needed, those objects are released. As they fall, a generator harnesses the energy created. Companies in Switzerland and Scotland are in the final stages of testing gravity storage plants, and it won't be long before others join them.

Building It Better

If we can build renewable energy plants and better storage capabilities for the power generated by these sources, why not think about what else we can build better? When we combine renewable energy sources with energy-efficient heating and cooling systems like those on the ISS, it's amazing what happens.

SMART HOUSES

In the Italian province of South Tyrol, an architect named Arthur Pichler built the country's first "passive" house. Found high in the Alps, the three-story house has no central heating system. It captures and stores all of its heat from the sun, and depends on excellent insulation to hang on to that heat when the temperatures get cold. It also helps keep the house cool when warmer summer weather comes around. The open-concept design—where only the bedrooms and bathrooms are closed off by doors—also makes sure the heat circulates evenly in the space.

Can't build an energy-smart home from the ground up? No problem. "Smart home" technologies are helping people cut down on energy use in their homes. Smart thermostats can be programmed to adjust heating and cooling depending on your needs. All tucked in for the night? The heat can probably be turned down. Away for the weekend? Set the thermostat so that the heat or air-conditioning comes on just before you get home. Smart light bulbs can be controlled by an app, which means there's no excuse for forgetting to turn off the light. And smart plugs can help you keep an eye on how much energy certain devices (such as televisions or computers) are using. The more information you have, the smarter you can be about your energy use.

SMART BUILDINGS

Like houses, buildings can also be designed with energy efficiency in mind. In southwestern Nigeria, where the average daytime temperature is about 33°C (90°F), Obafemi Awolowo University was purposely designed to keep students and staff cool. The campus features open gardens and courtyards that allow wind to move—a simple idea that keeps classrooms about 7°C (12.6°F) cooler than the air outside.

Small But Mighty

Thanks to research done for space-craft, solar panels are now highly efficient, making them a popular choice for some homeowners looking to create cleaner electricity. Newer solar panels are becoming so small and efficient that engineers are also working on solar-powered cars and airplanes. There are even portable solar panels you can hang from a backpack to charge your smartphone!

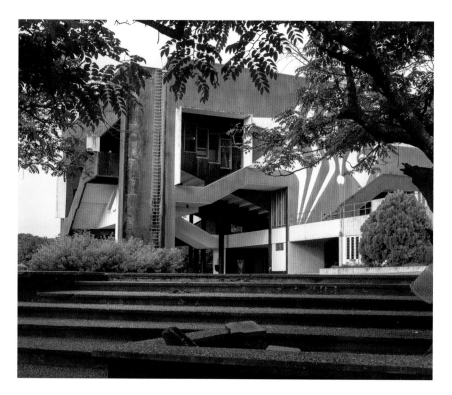

Obafemi Awolowo University, Ile-Ife, Nigeria

On the other side of the world, in Seattle, Washington, the Bullitt Center takes sustainability to the next level. The "greenest commercial building in the world" was designed to last 250 years (which is six times longer than most buildings). It collects and treats rainwater on-site, has a gray-water system, and uses composting toilets. It also has solar panels, pumps that use water warmed by Earth's core to provide additional heat, and a heat-recovery ventilation system that transfers warmth from outgoing air to the fresh incoming air. With all of this energy-efficient technology, it's no surprise that the Bullitt Center produces as much energy as it uses.

SMART CITIES

Entire cities can be smarter when it comes to energy efficiency, too. In Germany, Frankfurt is trying to reach climate neutrality by 2050. That means the city's greenhouse gas emissions would be no greater than the emissions that the planet's natural systems can remove. By asking scientists for help, city planners are coming up with ways to make this happen. Solar panels, biomass, and geothermal energy will help heat homes and buildings, taking some of the pressure off the city's power grid.

Frankfurt isn't alone. Each year, the Smart City Observatory releases a Smart City Index (SCI). In 2021, Singapore topped the list for the third year in a row. The government is trying to transform Singapore into a "city in a garden." It recently built a garden of solar-powered, artificial "supertrees"—stretching 50 meters (165 feet) into the sky—to collect solar power, act as air vents for nearby buildings, and harvest rainwater. Zurich and Oslo came in second and third, thanks to energy-efficient construction and transportation projects, and top-notch recycling efforts.

The highest-ranked U.S. city in the 2021 Smart City Index is New York, in the 12th spot, and Los Angeles sits at 31. In Canada, Vancouver comes in at 33, Toronto at 36, and Montreal at 38.

Singapore Supertrees at the Gardens by the Bay

Think Like an Astronaut

You may not be able to build an ISS-level solar array to create electricity, or even convince your parents or the building manager to put solar panels on the roof, but you can definitely reduce your use of electricity—and reliance on fossil fuels—in other ways.

Turn Off the Lights

Reducing the amount of electricity you use reduces your use of fossil fuels. A simple way to use less electricity at home is by turning off the lights when you aren't using them. You can also ask your parents to switch to more efficient LED lights, if they haven't already, and to make sure they turn off the lights, too. Just tell them that Cornell University in Ithaca, New York, calculated that it could save $60,000 a year by asking students and staff to turn off lights that aren't being used.

Unplug!

Don't stop at turning off the lights. Think for a minute about all the stuff in your house that's plugged in, even when it's not being used. We're talking about TVs, modems, computers, gaming systems, chargers for all of your devices, even appliances. Did you know that they use power even if they're turned off? This "phantom power" adds up to about $165 per household each year—which adds up to $19 million in the United States alone. It also causes 48 million tons of CO_2 to be released into the atmosphere. So, if you're not using it, pull the plug!

Ditch the Plastics

Say goodbye to single-use paper and plastic items (like napkins, straws, and plastic water bottles) and try cloth napkins, metal straws, and water bottles that you can refill instead. Manufacturing

just 1 kilogram (2.2 pounds) of the plastic used to make water bottles can produce 3 kilograms (6.6 pounds) of CO_2. If that doesn't sound like much, remember that, worldwide, we buy 1 million plastic bottles every minute.

Try Meatless Monday

In chapter 3, we learned how some indus-trial farming practices—including the ones that produce our meat—are high-carbon-footprint energy hogs. Enjoying a Meatless Monday every week could reduce the same amount of emis-sions created by driving 560 kilometers (348 miles) in the family

car each year. If the entire world reduced meat consumption by 15 percent, it would be like taking 240 million cars off the road every year.

Dust Off Your Sneakers

Did you know that close to 24 billion pairs of shoes are produced every year—and most of them are sneakers? Sneaker pro-duction accounts for 1.4 percent of the greenhouse gas emissions every year! If you think you need a new pair, maybe think again. Could you give them a good clean-ing and then take them for a walk to school? You'd be helping the planet save energy in two ways!

EXPERIMENTING WITH DR. DAVE

Testing Sun Power

The space station gets all of its energy from the sun, and the sun also produces electricity and heat on Earth. In this experiment, we'll learn more about how solar power works by creating a solar tower.

You'll need:

- three clean tin cans
- a can opener
- tape
- scissors
- safety scissors
- a paper straw

- two small blocks of wood about 2.5 cm (1 in.) high, 5 cm (2 in.) wide, and 10 cm (4 in.) long, or two hardcover books about that size
- a thumbtack
- a glue stick, a 10 cm (4 in.) square piece of paper

- a small bead that fits on the point of the thumbtack
- a sunny window. (optional)

1. Clean the cans, soak off the labels, and remove the bottoms with a can opener. Ask an adult to help you and to make sure there are no sharp edges when you are done.

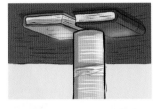

2. Tape the three cans together, top to bottom, to form a tower a little over 30 cm (1 ft) tall.

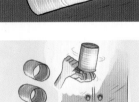

3. Place your wooden blocks or books side by side on a table, with about three fingers of space between them. Place your tower on top so it sits on the edge of each block. (There should be a space for air to flow under the tower and between the blocks).

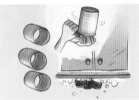

4. Now, we're going to use the rest of your materials to make a pinwheel. Using safety scissors, cut diagonally in from each corner of your piece of paper until you are about halfway to the center.

5. With the paper on a flat surface, use your glue stick to create a sticky spot in the center. Bend one side of a corner toward the center of the paper and stick it down firmly. Repeat this process for the other three corners. Now you have a pinwheel!

6. Find the spot halfway from the end of the straw. Carefully push the thumbtack through the center of the pinwheel and through the paper straw at this point. If you want, you can put a small bead between the pinwheel and the straw to help the pinwheel spin easily.

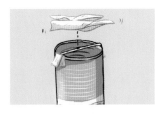

7. Lay the paper straw over the top of the tower so the pinwheel is in the center of the uppermost can. Then fold the paper straw down on each side of the can and tape each end to the top of the can so the pinwheel sits on top of the tower. Check to make sure your pinwheel can easily rotate.

8. Move your tower so it's sitting on its blocks by a window in bright sunlight.

9. Be patient and wait awhile.

What happens when the sun warms up the cans? You should see the pinwheel slowly starting to turn! When the air inside the cans is warmed by the sun, it rises and turns the pinwheel. The tower you made is called an updraft tower—as the warm air inside the tower rises, it sucks cooler air into the bottom of the tower. If there is sunlight to warm the cans, the wheel will keep turning.

THE FUTURE OF SUSTAINABILITY

Earth may be a whole lot bigger than the International Space Station, but if you've learned anything while reading this book, it's that the humans who live here and the astronauts who live there have some important things in common. For all of us, life as we know it depends on taking good care of our environment.

In space, the need to live in a sustainable way is only going to get more important in the coming years. NASA is already planning its next moon landing, set for 2025. Part of that mission's work will be to search out sites for the Artemis Base Camp—a future long-term home for astronauts doing research in space.

It's exciting to think about having a base we can visit on the moon, or even about the first human mission to Mars, but figuring out how to make those missions work is a big challenge. Mars is about 224 million kilometers (about 140 million miles) away from Earth. If you run out of clean air up there—or, say, milk—there's no one nearby to help. And a resupply ship would have to travel for seven months just to reach you. If you think sustainable living is a challenge on the ISS, you haven't seen anything yet!

But What about the Rockets?

In all of this talk about the future of space travel, we've left out a big question about sustainability: What about the energy it takes to get us into space in the first place?

Rocket launches use a lot of fuel—and not all of it is eco-friendly. A single launch can send between 200 and 300 tons of CO_2 into the atmosphere. That's similar to what would be produced by driving a car around the circumference of Earth between 20 and 28 times. With the number of rocket launches increasing every year, finding a better fuel is a priority.

When Blue Origin's *New Shepherd* lifted off in July 2021, it was powered by rocket fuel made up of liquid hydrogen and liquid oxygen. There was no carbon in the fuel, so no CO_2 was released when it burned up. Other pollutants were released, though, including nitrogen oxides and water vapor, and those can be damaging to the upper layers of Earth's atmosphere.

Companies like Blue Origin, SpaceX, and Virgin Galactic—as well as space agencies like NASA and the European Space Agency—are all trying to do better. Europe's biggest launch company, ArianeGroup, is hoping to launch a "carbon neutral" rocket in 2030. The plan is for it to run on methane produced from biomass (organic material like wood, plants, or manure). That would be another step in the right direction.

Thankfully, space agencies, companies, and researchers are working on projects that could make all of this possible (turn the page to find out more!). Could the technologies they are developing be as useful on Earth as they are on Mars or the moon? We'll have to wait and see!

Here are just a few of the exciting projects that could make space travel and life on Earth more sustainable in the future.

A Real Shower

In chapter 1, we learned that astronauts don't really shower in space, at least not the way we do on Earth. A "real" shower (as opposed to a sponge bath) wastes too much water in a system that has to conserve every drop it has. But what if all of that water going down the drain could be saved and reused? NASA, along with Lund University in Sweden, is working on a shower that recycles its water.

The system starts with less than 4.5 liters (1 gallon) of water. Water from regular showers has to be treated in a sewage treatment plant before it can be reused. The water in the space shower circulates much faster and at a higher rate, with a quality check taking place 20 times per second. Water unfit for circulation is removed, but the rest is filtered and then treated with ultraviolet light. Then it's back in circulation—cleaner than the water that comes out of our faucets at home.

Astronauts will definitely be excited about this technology, but it can also make a difference on Earth, where we need to keep making every drop count.

Breathing Easy on Mars

When the *Perseverance* rover landed on Mars in 2021, its main mission was to study the surface, looking for signs of microbial life in the planet's past. But the rover was also carrying equipment to test another project—an air filter that can convert carbon dioxide to oxygen by "breathing like a tree." The Mars Oxygen In-Situ Resource Utilization Experiment—or MOXIE—got the job done, capturing 10 minutes of breathable air from the red planet's environment. Much more testing is needed before Mars is safe for humans, but it's a promising start for a technology that could also help us breathe easier on Earth.

Grow Your Own Meat?

In 2019, Israel's Aleph Farms made an exciting announcement: they'd produced meat in space, without harming a single animal. Cow cells were harvested on Earth and sent to the ISS, where they were used to "grow" muscle tissue using a 3D bioprinter. Two weeks later, a strip of steak was ready to eat.

Although it didn't taste great, researchers considered the experiment a success. "In space, we don't have 10,000 or 15,000 liters [2,600 or 4,000 gallons] of water available to produce 1 kilogram [2 pounds] of beef," said Didier Toubia, from Aleph Farms. Lab-grown meat could help feed astronauts on future long-haul space missions, but it could also help feed Earth's growing population—providing food security while also conserving our natural resources.

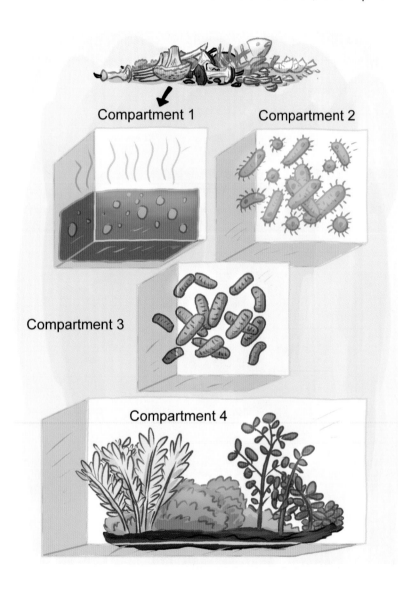

Compartment 1

Compartment 2

Compartment 3

Compartment 4

The European SpaceAgency's Micro-Ecological Life Support System Alternative (MELiSSA)

Waste to Food?

Getting rid of trash and waste in space is only going to get harder as journeys and stays get longer. Maybe MELiSSA can help. The European Space Agency's Micro-Ecological Life Support System Alternative takes the work done by the

Environmental Control and Life Support System (see pages 16–17 and 34–35) a few steps further. The team working on the technology calls it an "artificial ecosystem which uses microorganisms to process the waste so that we can grow plants."

Human and food waste travel through three compartments, where they are broken down through a process called fermentation (which uses microorganisms such as bacteria and yeasts and molds). In the fourth compartment, algae and plants are able to grow. Not only does this produce food, but it also helps exchange CO_2 for oxygen. MELiSSA isn't ready for space travel yet, but experiments are being planned for the ISS.

Space: Where the Sun Always Shines

Solar farms are becoming popular on Earth as we try to cut back on our use of fossil fuels. But some countries are taking the idea to a whole new level: space. China, for example, plans to launch a solar power plant into orbit by 2050. The energy captured—and there'd be a lot of it, since the sun always shines in space and there's no bad weather—would be beamed back to Earth for use by a growing population. Right now, China is testing ways to make that energy transfer work. Japan is also exploring the idea.

Take all these exciting space innovations in water, air, food, waste, and energy, add them to our big efforts here on Earth, and we can make living sustainably—now and in the future—a reality!

Glossary

aeroponics: a way of growing plants that uses no soil and only a little water. The roots of the plant hang in the air inside a container and are sprayed with a mist that has the nutrients they need to grow.

aerosols: tiny, floating dust particles and droplets in the air. Some aerosols are produced by nature (such as sand, salt, ice crystals, and ash from volcanos). Others are made by humans (such as pesticides, pollution, and soot and ash from fires).

atmosphere: the layer of gases that surround Earth (often called "air"). The atmosphere helps us stay warm and gives us the oxygen we breathe.

carbon dioxide (CO$_2$): a molecule that contains two oxygen atoms and one carbon atom. CO$_2$ is produced when we breathe and when we burn fossil fuels.

climate change: a change in the normal weather for a region over a long period of time. The phrase "climate change" is also used when talking about how Earth is heating up enough to melt glaciers, cause droughts, and put some species (including humans) at risk.

compost: a kind of fertilizer made when bacteria is used to break down rotting plants.

cosmonaut: a Russian astronaut.

electrolysis: a way of splitting substances by using an electric current. The ECLSS system on the International Space System uses electrolysis to separate water into hydrogen and oxygen (see pages 16 and 33).

emissions: gases that are released into the atmosphere. Right now, our greenhouse gas emissions (see page 31) are too high. This is a big factor when it comes to climate change and warming temperatures on Earth.

e-waste (electronic waste): anything we throw away that has plugs, cords, or electronic components (televisions, computers, and mobile phones, for example).

exosphere: the top layer of the Earth's atmosphere.

gravity: an invisible force that pulls objects toward each other. Without Earth's gravity, you'd have to be strapped down to keep your feet on the ground, and if you kicked a ball, it would never land. The sun's gravity keeps the Earth orbiting around the sun at just the right distance for life to survive—not too hot, and not too cold.

groundwater: water that is below the ground. Groundwater is an important part of the water cycle. The process starts when rain or snow falls to the ground and is absorbed into the earth. The water stays underground for a long time in aquifers (see page 22), and then returns to the surface through rivers and springs.

hydroponics: a way of growing plants without using soil. The nutrients the plants need are delivered to the roots in water.

microgravity: the condition in space when the effects of gravity are very small, and people or objects seem to be weightless. Microgravity is sometimes called "zero gravity," but this isn't correct—there is always a bit of gravity when you are orbiting a planet.

microorganism: living things (such as bacteria, viruses, and some molds) that are too small to be seen without a microscope. Although most microorganisms are essential to life on Earth, some of them are harmful and can cause disease.

oxygen: a colorless, odorless, tasteless gas that we breathe. Most life forms on Earth need oxygen to survive.

photosynthesis: the process by which plants use sunlight to create food from carbon dioxide and water. Oxygen is a by-product of photosynthesis.

reactor: a machine that uses nuclear energy to produce heat. The OSCAR system for changing space trash into water and gas has a reactor (see page 75).

renewable resource: a natural resource—such as air, water, or soil—that cannot be used up or that can be replaced within the lifespan of a human.

sanitation: the process of keeping things free from filth, infection, and other dangers to human health, such as feces and urine. Sanitation practices include disposing of garbage, treating wastewater, and managing hazardous waste. Sanitation is important because it helps prevent the spread of germs and diseases.

satellite: a small object that revolves around a larger object in space. Satellites can be natural (like the moon), or human made, like the ones launched into space to gather information.

solar radiation: the sunlight and energy that comes from the sun and travels to Earth in the form of light waves.

sustainability: the idea that we need to take care of our environment so that there will be resources left for future generations. Sustainable living means thinking carefully about how we use food, water, and plants, and what we put into the environment.

upcycling: taking something that would normally be trash or recycling and turning it into something better.

water cycle: the way water moves around the Earth through evaporation, condensation, and precipitation. Water evaporates from the surface of the Earth and rises into the atmosphere. Once there, it cools and condenses into rain or snow in clouds, and then falls back to Earth as precipitation. It collects in lakes and rivers, in soil, and even in layers of rock. Eventually, most of it evaporates again and the cycle continues.

Selected Sources

INTRODUCTION

Howell, Elizabeth. "International Space Station: Facts about the Orbital Laboratory." Space.com, August 24, 2022. https://www.space.com/16748-international-space-station.html

Sommer, Lauren. "This Is What the World Looks Like if We Pass the Crucial 1.5-degree Climate Threshold." NPR, November 8, 2021. https://www.npr.org/2021/11/08/1052198840/1-5-degrees-warming-climate-change

"Vital Signs: Global Temperature." NASA: Global Climate Change, n.d. https://climate.nasa.gov/vital-signs/global-temperature/

CHAPTER 1

Chow, Denise. "Everyday Tech from Space: Water Recyclers Make Pee Potable." Space.com, January 31, 2011. https://www.space.com/10725-space-spinoff-technology-water-recycling.html

"Distance Learning Module: Recycling Water in Space." McAuliffe-Shepard Discovery Center, May 26, 2020. https://www.starhop.com/blog/2020/5/26/distance-learning-module-recycling-water-9b42j

"Drip Calculator." American Water Works Association, n.d. https://drinktap.org/water-info/water-conservation/drip-calculator

"Food Facts: How Much Water Does It Take to Produce...?" Water Education Foundation, n.d. https://www.watereducation.org/post/food-facts-how-much-water-does-it-take-produce

Johnson, Michael, ed. "Advanced NASA Technology Supports Water Purification Efforts Worldwide." NASA, October 9, 2019. https://www.nasa.gov/mission_pages/station/research/news/b4h-3rd/it-advanced-nasa-water-purification

Lewis, Angela. "Satellite Serves a Thirstier World." SSPI.org, June 17, 2013. https://www.sspi.org/cpages/satellite-serves-a-thirstier-world

Manganello, Kristin. "Which Industries Use the Most Water?" Thomas, March 22, 2019. https://www.thomasnet.com/insights/which-industries-use-the-most-water/

"NASA Facts International Space System Environmental Control and Life Support." NASA: Marshall Space Flight Center, December 2004. https://www.nasa.gov/centers/marshall/pdf/174687main_eclss_facts.pdf

"Water Facts of Life." Environmental Protection Agency, n.d. https://www3.epa.gov/safewater/kids/waterfactsoflife.html

"Water on the Space Station." NASA Science, November 2, 2000. https://science.nasa.gov/science-news/science-at-nasa/2000/ast02nov_1

CHAPTER 2

"10 Interesting Things about Air." NASA, Climate Kids, n.d. https://climatekids.nasa.gov/10-things-air/

"Air Pollution." World Health Organization, n.d. https://www.who.int/health-topics/air-pollution#tab=tab_1

"Air Quality and Health." World Health Organizataion, n.d. https://www.who.int/airpollution/ambient/health-impacts/en/

"Ambient (Outdoor) Air Pollution." World Health Organization. September 22, 2021. https://www.who.int/news-room/fact-sheets/detail/ambient-(outdoor)-air-quality-and-health

"Eating in Space." Canada.ca, n.d. https://www.asc-csa.gc.ca/eng/astronauts/living-in-space/eating-in-space.asp

Hall, Melanie "Feeding the World of the Future: Is Hydroponics the Answer?" DW, May 18, 2018. https://www.dw.com/en/feeding-the-world-of-the-future-is-hydroponics-the-answer/g-43838731

"History of Hydroponics." The Natural Farmer, n.d. https://thenaturalfarmer.org/article/the-history-of-hydroponics/

"Household Air Pollution and Health." World Health Organization, July 27, 2022. https://www.who.int/news-room/fact-sheets/detail/household-air-pollution-and-health

"Hunger and Food Insecurity." Food and Agricultural Organization of the United Nations, n.d. http://www.fao.org/hunger/en/

"What Is the AQI?" Air Now, n.d. https://www.airnow.gov/education/students/what-is-the-aqi/

CHAPTER 3

Ayer, Paula, and Antonia Banyard. *Eat Up! An Infographic Exploration of Food*. Toronto: Annick Press, 2017.

Breene, Keith. "Food Security and Why It Matters." World Economic Forum, January 18, 2016. https://www.weforum.org/agenda/2016/01/food-security-and-why-it-matters/

Brown, Michael J. "Curious Kids: Where Does the Oxygen on the International Space Station Come from and Why Don't They Run Out of Air." The Conversation, December 5, 2017. https://theconversation.com/curious-kids-where-does-the-oxygen-come-from-in-the-international-space-station-and-why-dont-they-run-out-of-air-82910

Chaturvedi, Aditya. "How Satellites Are Changing the Way We Track Pollution on the Ground." The Wire, July 30, 2019. https://thewire.in/environment/how-satellites-are-changing-the-way-we-track-pollution-on-the-ground

Elferink, Maarten, and Florian Schierhorn. "Global Demand for Food Is Rising. Can We Meet It?" *Harvard Business Review*, April 7, 2016. https://hbr.org/2016/04/global-demand-for-food-is-rising-can-we-meet-it

McFadden, Christopher. "15+ Projects That Could End Air Pollution around the World." Interesting Engineering, September 12, 2020. https://interestingengineering.com/15-projects-that-could-end-air-pollution-around-the-world

Robinson, Deena. "25 Shocking Facts about Food Waste." Earth.org, September 29, 2022. https://earth.org/facts-about-food-waste/

Roser, Max, and Hannah Ritchie. "Hunger and Undernourishment." Our World in Data, n.d. https://ourworldindata.org/hunger-and-undernourishment

CHAPTER 4

"Biogas Facts for Kids." Kiddle, n.d. https://kids.kiddle.co/Biogas

Choi, Candice. "17% of Food Produced Globally Wasted Every Year, U.N. Report Estimates." Global News, March 4, 2021. https://globalnews.ca/news/7676470/global-food-waste-un-report/

Eamer, Claire. *What a Waste! Where Does Garbage Go*? Toronto: Annick Press, 2017.

"From Trash to Cash in Saint-Michel." CBC News, October 16, 2017. https://www.cbc.ca/news/canada/montreal/turning-garbage-into-clean-energy-1.4357531

Gohd, Chelsea. "NASA's Big Astronaut Trash Problem." Space.com, July 12, 2018. https://www.space.com/41131-nasa-tackles-astronaut-trash-problem.html

Harvey, Fiona. "Mismanaged Waste, Kills up to a Million People a Year Globally," *The Guardian*, May 14, 2019. https://www.theguardian.com/environment/2019/may/14/mismanaged-waste-kills-up-to-a-million-people-a-year-globally

Mingle, Jonathan. "Could Renewable Natural Gas Be the Next Big Thing in Green Energy?" Yale Environment 360, July 25, 2019. https://e360.yale.edu/features/could-renewable-natural-gas-be-the-next-big-thing-in-green-energy

"NASA Technology Designed to Turn Space Trash into Treasure." NASA, June 5, 2020. https://www.nasa.gov/spacetech/NASA_Technology_Designed_to_Turn_Space_Trash_into_Treasure

Thompson, Derek. "2.6 Trillion Pounds of Garbage: Where Does the World's trash Go?" *The Atlantic*, June 26, 2012. https://www.theatlantic.com/business/archive/2012/06/26-trillion-pounds-of-garbage-where-does-the-worlds-trash-go/258234/

"What Is NASA's Heat Melt Compactor?" NASA, August 16, 2018. https://www.nasa.gov/ames/heat-melt-compactor

CHAPTER 5

Campbell, Maeve. "Which Country Is the World Leader in Renewable Energy in 2021?" Euronews.Green, August 16, 2021. https://www.euronews.com/green/2021/08/02/which-country-is-the-world-leader-in-renewable-energy-in-2021

Gray, Richard. "The Biggest Energy Challenges Facing Humanity." BBC, March 13, 2017. https://www.bbc.com/future/article/20170313-the-biggest-energy-challenges-facing-humanity

"Fossil Fuel Facts for Kids." Kidz Feed, n.d. https://kidzfeed.com/fossil-fuels-facts-for-kids/

"Fossil Fuels" National Geographic Resource Library, May 20, 2022. https://www.nationalgeographic.org/encyclopedia/fossil-fuels/

"History of Solar Energy." Energysage, n.d. https://news.energysage.com/the-history-and-invention-of-solar-panel-technology/

"Lithium-Ion Batteries Need to Be Greener and More Ethical." Nature, June 29, 2021. https://www.nature.com/articles/d41586-021-01735-z

"New Solar Arrays to Power NASA's International Space Station Research." NASA, January 11, 2021. https://www.nasa.gov/feature/new-solar-arrays-to-power-nasa-s-international-space-station-research

Paleja, Shaker. *Power Up! A Visual Exploration of Energy*. Toronto: Annick Press, 2015.

"Top 19 Biggest Solar Plants in the World." Solar Feeds, October 7, 2021. https://www.solarfeeds.com/mag/solar-farms-in-the-world/

"Wind Power." Kids Britannica, n.d. https://kids.britannica.com/kids/article/wind-power/574607

CONCLUSION

Associated Press, "NASA Delays Astronaut Moon Landing, Plans to Miss Deadline," CBC News, November 10, 2021. https://www.cbc.ca/news/science/nasa-moon-landing-1.6243833

Chow, Denise, and Alyssa Newcomb. "Solar Farms in Space Could Be Renewable Energy's Next Frontier." NBC News, March 9, 2019. https://www.nbcnews.com/mach/science/solar-farms-space-could-be-renewable-energy-s-next-frontier-ncna967451

Clifford, Tyler. "Lydall Testing Air Filters to Convert CO_2 into Oxygen on Mars with NASA Rover, CEO Says." CNBC, May 3, 2021. https://www.cnbc.com/2021/05/03/lydall-testing-air-filters-to-convert-co2-into-oxygen-on-mars-with-nasa-rover-ceo-says.html

"Greenhouse Gas Equivalencies Calculator." United States Environmental Protection Agency, n.d. https://www.epa.gov/energy/greenhouse-gas-equivalencies-calculator

"Mission Timeline: Cruise," NASA Science, n.d. https://mars.nasa.gov/mars2020/timeline/cruise/

"MOXIE." NASA Science, n.d. https://mars.nasa.gov/mars2020/spacecraft/instruments/moxie/

"NASA Outlines Lunar Surface Sustainability Concept." NASA, April 2, 2020. https://www.nasa.gov/feature/nasa-outlines-lunar-surface-sustainability-concept

Smithers, Rebecca. "First Meat Grown in Space Lab 248 Miles from Earth." *The Guardian*, October 7, 2019. https://www.theguardian.com/environment/2019/oct/07/wheres-the-beef-248-miles-up-as-first-meat-is-grown-in-a-space-lab

"Space-Age Water Conservation." NASA Spinoff, July 13, 2021. https://spinoff.nasa.gov/page/space-age-water-conservation-nasa

"Waste Not, Want Not on the Road to Mars." European Space Agency, July 26, 2001. https://www.esa.int/Science_Exploration/Human_and_Robotic_Exploration/Exploration/Waste_not_want_not_on_the_road_to_Mars

Image Sources

TITLE PAGE AND CHAPTER OPENER BACKGROUNDS:
hanohiki / iStock / Getty Images

INTRODUCTION
6 Johnson Space Center / NASA; **7** Dave Reede / All Canada Photos; **8** David Burdick / NOAA; **9** Canadian Space Agency, 2019

CHAPTER 1
10 Jet Propulsion Laboratory / NASA; **14** Johnson Space Center / NASA; 18, **26**, **27** (background) klyaksun / Shutterstock;
20 Thomas Peter / REUTERS / Alamy Stock Photo; **23** Joe Marino-Bill Cantrell/UPI / Alamy Stock Photo

CHAPTER 2
28 Johnson Space Center / NASA; **34 tl** Bakavets Sviatlana / Shutterstock; **tr** Gines Valera Marin / Shutterstock;
b (from l to r) Azat Valeev / Shutterstock; honglouwawa / Shutterstock; honglouwawa / Shutterstock; **36** Johnson Space Center
/ NASA; **37**, **38**, **43**, **47** (background) Vivek Toshniwal / Shutterstock; **46** Chih Yuan Wu / Dreamstime.com

CHAPTER 3
48 Anna Kucherova / Shutterstock; **51** M. Niebuhr / Shutterstock; **53**, **56** (background) Vadim Gromov / Unsplash;
57 Johnson Space Center / NASA; **63** siswoto/Shutterstock; **64 t** Photo courtesy of Arctic Research Foundation. Naurvik
is operated in partnership with Arctic Research Foundation, Agriculture and Agri-Food Canada, Canadian Space Agency,
the National Research Council, and the community of Gjoa Haven; **b** Opachevsky Irina / Shutterstock;
66 Peter Bennett / Citizen of the Planet / Alamy Stock Photo

CHAPTER 4
68 dottedhippo/iStock; **72**, **74**, **75** (background) j.chizhe / Shutterstock; **74** Johnson Space Center / NASA;
75 NASA/Ames Research Center/Dominic Hart; **82** ESA / ATG medialab; **84** Wirestock Creators / Shutterstock

CHAPTER 5
86 Johnson Space Center / NASA; **88** Dominik Vanyi / Unsplash; **90** Pstedrak / Dreamstime.com; **92**, **93** Johnson Space Center /
NASA; **97** Johnson Space Center/NASA; **101** Ikochet / Dreamstime.com; **102** ERIMIPO SEGUN-OKEOWO / Shutterstock;
103 Svetlana Day / Dreamstime.com; **105** Warren Jones / Unsplash; **108** Image created by Reto Stöckli, Nazmi El Saleous, and
Marit Jentoft-Nilsen, NASA GSFC; **109** Blue Origin / Alamy Stock Photo; **113** Andreas Gucklhorn/Unsplash

Index